Cover Letters
In A Week

Patricia Scudamore & Hilton Catt

20 14002 747

NEW COLLEGE, SWINDON

Patricia Scudamore and Hilton Catt have many years' experience of working in recruitment, enabling them to bring the perspective of both employer and candidate. They have written over 25 books based on their experience of what it takes to make careers work in today's rapidly changing and uncertain world. They were among the first to embrace the idea of people taking on the job of managing their own careers as opposed to leaving it to employers to do the thinking for them. They have seen for themselves the richness and diversity modern careers can offer and one of the central themes in their work is exploiting this richness and diversity to the full. They have written a number of other books in the Teach Yourself series. You can visit their website at scudamorecatt.com and their blog site at patriciascudamorehiltoncatt.com

Teach Yourself ®

Cover Letters In A Week

Patricia Scudamore & Hilton Catt

2014002747

First published in Great Britain in 2013 by Hodder Education

This edition published in 2016 by John Murray Learning

Copyright © Patricia Scudamore and Hilton Catt 2013, 2016

The rights of Patricia Scudamore and Hilton Catt to be identified as the Authors of the Work has been asserted by them in accordance with the Copyright, Designs and Patents Act 1988.

Database right Hodder & Stoughton (makers)

The *Teach Yourself* name is a registered trademark of Hachette UK.

All rights reserved. No part of this publication may be reproduced, stored in a retrieval system or transmitted in any form or by any means, electronic, mechanical, photocopying, recording or otherwise, without the prior written permission of the publisher, or as expressly permitted by law, or under terms agreed with the appropriate reprographic rights organization. Enquiries concerning reproduction outside the scope of the above should be sent to the Rights Department, John Murray Learning, at the address below.

You must not circulate this book in any other binding or cover and you must impose this same condition on any acquirer.

British Library Cataloguing in Publication Data: a catalogue record for this title is available from the British Library.

ISBN 9781473609426

eISBN 9781444185812

1

The publisher has used its best endeavours to ensure that any website addresses referred to in this book are correct and active at the time of going to press. However, the publisher and the author have no responsibility for the websites and can make no guarantee that a site will remain live or that the content will remain relevant, decent or appropriate.

The publisher has made every effort to mark as such all words which it believes to be trademarks. The publisher should also like to make it clear that the presence of a word in the book, whether marked or unmarked, in no way affects its legal status as a trademark.

Every reasonable effort has been made by the publisher to trace the copyright holders of material in this book. Any errors or omissions should be notified in writing to the publisher, who will endeavour to rectify the situation for any reprints and future editions.

Typeset by Cenveo® Publisher Services.

Printed and bound in Great Britain by CPI Group (UK) Ltd., Croydon, CR0 4YY.

John Murray Learning policy is to use papers that are natural, renewable and recyclable products and made from wood grown in sustainable forests. The logging and manufacturing processes are expected to conform to the environmental regulations of the country of origin.

Carmelite House
50 Victoria Embankment
London EC4 0DZ
www.hodder.co.uk

Also available
in ebook

Contents

Introduction

Over the course of the coming week we are going to teach you everything you need to know about:

- putting together a good cover letter
- understanding the important part cover letters play in moving job applications to successful conclusions
- how to use this knowledge to your advantage.

Starting on Sunday, read the book a chapter a day so over the week you will build up an expert appreciation of what it takes to make cover letters work for you across a wide range of situations.

On **Sunday** we will look at how important it is to make a good first impression and the vital part cover letters have to play in getting job applications off to a good start.

Cover letters are what employers read first. If what they see interests them, they'll look at your CV. If, on the other hand, they see nothing that interests them they might give your CV a miss, meaning that's the end of the road as far as your chances of getting the job are concerned. The impact your cover letter makes is, therefore, vital. We will also be looking at the importance of correct grammar and spelling and how to avoid your application going nowhere for this reason alone.

On **Monday** we will consider how all employers are different. What interests one won't necessarily interest another and catering for this diversity is important. At the same time we will show what you can do to make your cover letters 'employer friendly', which is the start of the all-important process of making employers want to engage with you.

Then on to **Tuesday** when we will look at what you need to put in a cover letter and how to set it out in a way which will be both (a) acceptable to the recipient and (b) eye-catching.

There are dos and don'ts to follow. There are different dos and don'ts for cover letters that are going to be emailed.

Unless you happen to work in some highly specialized field, jobs which have been advertised on the open or 'visible' market are going to draw in large numbers of applicants. On **Wednesday** we will show you how to design a cover letter specifically for the purpose of engaging and overcoming competition.

Thursday, on the other hand, will focus on the tricky job of designing a speculative cover letter for the 'invisible' market. Unsolicited job applications call for a more thought-out approach and we will tell you what works and what doesn't.

On **Friday** we will look at cover letters for registering with recruitment consultants (agencies) – people who will try to find a job for you but where the challenge is making sure they understand what you want.

Finally, on **Saturday,** we will look at how, with practice, you can learn and get better at writing cover letters.

THE LIBRARY
WITHDRAWN
NEW COLLEGE
SWINDON

SUNDAY

Making a good first impression

Today you will learn about good first impressions and why it is important to make them.

Cover letters occupy a special place in the stages through which a job application passes on its journey from you seeing an opportunity that interests you to what you hope will be a successful conclusion. Cover letters are what employers read first. Up to when your letter comes out of the envelope or arrives in an email, employers know nothing about you. They have no preconceived opinions on your suitability for the job, so the stage is set for you to convince them that it is you and not any of the others they should be taking seriously.

A simplified view of cover letters is that they act as appetisers. If your cover letter does its job, your CV gets read. If your CV does its job, you get an interview, and so on. However, what this simplified view fails to take into account is how well-written cover letters can go on working for you right the way through to the final stages of selection. We will explain how this happens as we take you through today's lesson.

The halo effect

If you have read another of our books in this series (*Job Applications In A Week*) you will already know about the halo effect.

The halo effect is the tendency to see some good points in a candidate at the start of the selection process and, from there on, to ignore any flaws which come to light. Professional interviewers are taught to beware of halo effects. They can lead to the wrong candidate getting the job.

The halo effect in reverse

What a lot of people don't realize is that the halo effect can work the other way round. Bad points can register at the beginning and, from there on, it is quite hard to make a comeback.

First impressions stick

The halo effect teaches us:

1 the importance of first impressions
2 how first impressions stick
3 how, once first impressions are formed, they are very hard to shift.

First impressions and cover letters

Cover letters occupy a unique place. They are what employers read first, so how they are seen, good or bad, will play an important part in determining what happens next. For example, a cover letter which arrives written on a scruffy piece of paper and full of spelling mistakes might mean the CV which accompanies it ends up being thrown in the bin without being read. Even if the CV does get a reading, an impression has already formed in the employer's mind and it hardly needs saying the impression won't be favourable and could be a strong factor in deciding who goes on the interview list and who doesn't.

Anyone who has worked in recruitment will tell you how common it is to find CVs which have had a lot of thought put into their preparation accompanied by cover letters which look like they've been dashed off in five minutes without anyone bothering to check them. In some cases it is difficult to believe the cover letters and CVs have been written by the same person.

Key point

It's no use spending hours crafting a great CV unless you are prepared to put the same level of time and effort into crafting an equally great cover letter. The two go together. One without the other doesn't work.

Make the most of the opportunity

There are still people out there who feel they can dispense with cover letters. They send in job applications attached to business cards or to home-made compliments slips. Alternatively, the cover letters they write consist of no more than a simple sentence or two, such as 'I wish to apply for the position of [ ]. A copy of my CV is enclosed. Yours sincerely'.

7

How such applications are received depends to a large extent on who reads them. Some employers may take the view that the person who sent in the application couldn't take the trouble to write a cover letter (a proper one); that would be a bad first impression. However, there is a much bigger point to be made here and it is this. A cover letter is an **opportunity** to make a good first impression, and missing the opportunity is a pity. Particularly in competitive situations (where jobs have been widely advertised and where there will be hundreds of other applicants), the need to score good first impressions is vital, and what better place to do it than in a cover letter?

An integral part of your CV

This is important. See your cover letter as an integral part of your CV – the front page, if you like. As we shall see later in the week, a cover letter serves the function of drawing out and précising the key points in your CV vis-à-vis the job for which you are applying. Like the front page of a newspaper, you are saying to your readers 'These are the headlines but you'll find lots more interesting stuff inside.'

Key point

In the business of getting jobs see a great cover letter and a great CV as the winning team.

How a cover letter goes on working for you

We have seen how good first impressions have a vital part to play in moving job applications forward. We have seen how, once you've made good first impressions, they stay there and go on working for you. What we also need to consider is that, as a job application progresses, it brings in more and more people. For example, if you get put on a short list, the Human Resources Manager who saw you at the first interview

SUNDAY

MONDAY

TUESDAY

WEDNESDAY

THURSDAY

FRIDAY

SATURDAY

will hand your papers over to another manager (perhaps the person who will be your boss if you get the job). The top item on your papers will be your cover letter, so now a fresh pair of eyes will be looking at it – someone else whose first impressions of what they see need to be good.

Bad English

Cover letters full of spelling mistakes, bad grammar, incorrect word usage and apostrophes in the wrong place don't go down well with employers. Now is perhaps an opportune moment to say a few words about how much damage job applicants inflict on themselves by not paying sufficient attention to their English.

When all is said and done, it is the responsibility of each one of us to make sure that anything we put in a cover letter (or, for that matter, a CV) projects an image which is consistent with the one we want to project. What we don't want to be seen as is someone who is careless or doesn't have the capacity to pay attention to detail, but sadly this is how cover letters and CVs riddled with mistakes come across. The people who put them together couldn't be bothered to check them properly and, to an employer, this doesn't say a lot for how the same people are going to get on when they're given some real responsibilities.

Later in the week we will be coming back to the subject of making sure that what you're writing won't be sending shudders down the spines of employers who read it!

Spellcheckers

There is nothing wrong with spellcheckers but people can and do place too much reliance on them. A survey recently commissioned by the learning disability charity Mencap highlighted the fact that spellcheckers have given many people a false impression of their spelling ability. Because they've used the spellchecker they think anything they write is fine. They don't proofread, they don't get out the dictionary, they don't go to the trouble of getting a second opinion and the result is they let themselves down badly. The even bigger problem for these people is that no one ever tells them why their applications keep on ending up on the reject pile. They go on sending in letters and CVs riddled with mistakes.

> ## Warning!
>
> Don't run away with the idea that the problem of letters and CVs full of mistakes is confined to school-leavers and recent graduates. On the contrary, we see many examples of letters written by well-qualified professionals, people applying for senior and top management jobs, which are equally bad.
>
> **Footnote:** the grammar and sentence construction in some cover letters is so bad they don't make sense.

Standard cover letters

We have already looked at cover letters consisting of nothing other than 'Please see attached CV'. Almost as bad – for reasons we'll explain shortly – is the sort of standard cover letter people keep in template form in the documents stored on their computer. Even worse is the standard letter which is printed off with blank spaces which people then fill in with their not always terribly tidy handwriting.

What's wrong with standard cover letters?

Apart from the usual opening and closing paragraphs, they typically give a thumbnail sketch of the applicant: e.g. qualifications, background, current employment, main responsibilities. The constraints of keeping the letter to one page of A4 then tend to kick in, so the employer reading it sees nothing that's greatly relevant to the position they're seeking to fill. Once again the opportunity to score points is missed and the cover letter and the CV that goes with it stand a fair chance of ending up on the same pile as those of all the other applicants who don't seem to have anything interesting to offer.

To employers who see a lot of job applications, standard cover letters:

● are instantly recognizable
● suggest minimal effort has gone into preparing them
● project an image of someone who doesn't overexert themselves
● project an image (perhaps) of someone who is applying for jobs all the time, i.e. not the kind of person who will be a long-term asset to the business.

Again, tomorrow's lesson will have a lot more to say about making cover letters do what you want them to do. A prominent message will be the need to engage employers with what interests them, not bland personal statements of the kind which will make them want to switch off.

Pay attention to detail

To people who have never worked in recruitment, it may be surprising to learn just how many cover letters come in with the name of the people to whom they're addressed spelt incorrectly or similar mistakes in the spelling of the names of businesses and/or their addresses. We say surprising because, in the majority of cases, all the applicant had to do was copy what appeared in an advertisement.

Since there can be no other explanation for these lapses apart from carelessness, the message here is always, always pay attention to detail. Needless to say, people who make silly mistakes don't endear themselves to employers. In the world of business, silly mistakes cost money.

Using your cover letter to project a good first impression

So what you need to focus on when you design a cover letter is the impact it will make when it lands on someone's desk. Will it make a good first impression? Or will it let you down and put the kiss of death on your application?

Here is a list of dos and don'ts on presentation which will help you

- to avoid some of the more common mistakes people make
- to ensure your cover letters make a good first impression when they arrive at their destination.

Do use black ink on standard white A4 paper.

Don't use coloured ink or paper because neither looks good if for any reason your cover letter has to be faxed or photocopied. The same goes for email, where some of the businesses you write to might print your letter off on a black and white printer.

Don't handwrite cover letters. It looks old-fashioned and, more importantly, you lose the capacity to draft, edit and make corrections.

Do stick to conventional fonts such as Arial or Times New Roman.

Don't try to catch employers' eyes by using fancy fonts and graphics. Keep it plain and simple.

Don't, in your efforts to get everything on one sheet of paper, try to save space by resorting to font sizes which will have your readers searching for their glasses (or conversely not bothering).

Do take care when printing off, especially on inkjet printers, where blots and smudges can become a problem.

Do take care with where you store the paper you use for your cover letters (and CVs). A waft of stale cigarette smoke or the smell of last night's fry-up as it comes out of the envelope at the other end won't do much for you on the first impressions front.

Do use a standard A4 white envelope.

Don't fold your cover letter and CV to make them fit in a small envelope. They will forever bear the crease marks and it runs the risk of someone at the other end with a not too clean pair of hands trying to smooth them out.

Do keep it concise. Achieve conciseness by keeping it relevant.

Do stick to the default settings when it comes to the width of margins or the spaces at the top and bottom of pages.

Don't try to squeeze more in by using every square centimetre of space available.

Do leave a clear line space between each of your paragraphs.

Don't try to cram more in by cutting down on white space.

Do remember to sign it.

Note: there will be more on setting out cover letters when we get to Tuesday.

Conclusion

SUNDAY

MONDAY

TUESDAY

WEDNESDAY

THURSDAY

FRIDAY

SATURDAY

Making a good first impression will set your job applications off on the right track. Today we have been looking at how cover letters, written with some thought and effort, are the starting point of a process which will hopefully end with you walking away with the offer of a job in your hand. The role of cover letters is often misunderstood. They are seen as serving no purpose other than providing the anchor point for attaching your CV. As a result, little attention is paid to what goes in them and a golden opportunity is missed for scoring important points right at the very start. An opportunity has also been missed for the same points to keep finding their mark with people who come into the selection process later on and who, by definition, will have a large say in whether you get the job or not.

Also today you have seen how silly mistakes in cover letters can and do put employers off. The mistakes stick out like a sore thumb and are in most cases the result of carelessness and failure to check letters properly before they are emailed or put in the post. The idea is for people to catch employers' eyes with their skills and abilities, not their bad grammar and spelling mistakes!

Fact-check (answers at the back)

1. What is special about a cover letter?
a) It is optional ❑
b) It saves having to write a CV ❑
c) It is what employers read first ❑
d) It guarantees getting a reply ❑

2. What is the halo effect?
a) The tendency to look for a candidate's good points ❑
b) The impact you can create by arriving for an interview smartly dressed ❑
c) The tendency to see good points in a candidate at the start of a selection process and thereafter to ignore any flaws that come out ❑
d) The effect when one candidate for a job is streets ahead of the others ❑

3. With which of these statements do you agree?
a) A cover letter is more important than a CV ❑
b) A CV is more important than a cover letter ❑
c) They are both as important as one another ❑
d) It depends on the job ❑

4. What is wrong with sending in a CV clipped to a compliments slip and without a cover letter?
a) It makes you look lazy ❑
b) You miss the opportunity to make a good first impression ❑
c) You won't get a reply ❑
d) There is nothing wrong with it ❑

5. In a cover letter, which will damage your chances of getting the job?
a) Spelling mistakes ❑
b) Getting the employer's name wrong ❑
c) Bad grammar ❑
d) All three of them ❑

6. Who is to blame for bad spelling in job applications?
a) The people who make the mistakes ❑
b) The education system ❑
c) Spellcheckers ❑
d) Nobody ❑

7. When is it acceptable to send in a CV without a cover letter?
a) When you need to get a job application off in a hurry ❑
b) When you've got a great CV ❑
c) When you're applying for a temporary position ❑
d) It is never acceptable ❑

8. What is the best way of making your cover letter stand out?
a) Printing it on bright coloured paper ❑
b) Keeping it interesting, concise and relevant ❑
c) Sending it by courier ❑
d) Putting your photograph on it ❑

9. What is the best way of making sure your cover letter has got no spelling mistakes in it?
a) Run the spellchecker over it more than once ❏
b) Check it carefully ❏
c) Your spelling is perfect so there is no need to do anything ❏
d) Look up any long words in the dictionary ❏

10. What is wrong with using the same cover letter every time you write off for a job?
a) It looks lazy ❏
b) There is nothing wrong with it ❏
c) Most of the letter won't be relevant to the job for which you are applying ❏
d) Don't know ❏

MONDAY

Making it work for you

Yesterday we looked at how cover letters can project a good first impression. Today we are going to look at what to put in them to get the right result.

A cover letter which does its job is one which prompts the reader to want to find out more.

It sounds simple and to some extent it is. Readers of cover letters (employers with positions they need to fill) want to find applicants who tick the boxes. Forget, therefore, the image of employers as people who don't read anything that doesn't jump off the page at them. Yes, most of them are busy people with all sorts of conflicting demands on their time but, if they see an application come in which offers a solution to a problem which is causing them pain (such as a hole in the ranks), then they're hooked. The tricky part, as you've probably guessed, is convincing the employers that you offer the solution and to do it in a cover letter. This is what we'll be focussing on today.

What we'll also be looking at is what it takes to make yourself 'employer friendly'. 'Employer friendly' means having the capacity to put yourself in employers' shoes, seeing it the way they see it and helping them with the job they have to do. The job in this case is sifting through applications to find ones which are suitable.

The 'one quick read' test

Though all employers are different in the way they process job applications, cover letters do in many cases have to survive quite robust treatment. Here it is worth noting that:

- Reading cover letters sometimes consists of little more than a quick flick through.
- Cover letters are not always read from start to finish.
- Cover letters are rarely read twice (once they've been put on the reject pile they tend to stay there).

What this means, especially in competitive job situations, is:

- What you have to offer has got to come across first time (it may not get another chance).
- What you have to offer has got to match up with what the employer wants.

Defining the message

So what are employers looking for? Which of your attributes will be the most compelling when it comes to booking your place on the interview list?

No one size fits all

All employers are different. Take two manufacturing businesses looking for someone to head up their human resources management teams. Business A is highly unionized and practically everything is determined by collective bargaining. Business B, on the other hand, is run on paternalistic lines with little union involvement and the main function of human resources management is to administer various welfare schemes. Experience as a hard-nosed negotiator would probably figure highly on the list of key attributes of the job with Business A whereas, with Business B, it would probably not.

> ## Key point
>
> The tendency to think employers see things the same way is a common mistake in cover letters (and CVs). They do not. What is a 'must have' attribute to one won't necessarily be the same to another. This brings us back to the subject of standard cover letters we touched on yesterday. Repeating the same information over and over again every time you send off a job application won't win you many friends.

Look at the ad for the job

So, given this diversity, how do you go about finding out what employers want? Where do you look to discover what they will find interesting?

A good starting place is the ad for the job, which tells you in outline terms what the employer sees as key qualities. Sometimes the ad will tell you how you can access a full-blown job specification, for example by downloading it from a website.

Where else to look for clues to employers' thinking

Ads, of course, don't tell you everything. They rarely, for example, tell you anything about the culture of businesses or other information which would give you some clues to their preferences when it comes to the people they take on.

Suggestions on where else to look?

- **The Internet** is an obvious place. In addition to employers' own websites, you can tap into other interesting insights by searching round; for example, recent news items or, pushing the boundaries a little further, social networking sites.
- **Use your professional networks.** If you have been active in a career for a number of years you will have built up a circle of contacts who may be able to offer you some inside information. Best of all are contacts who work for the employer or who have worked for them in the past.

Make your strong points stand out

So, to summarize, what we have done so far is look at what employers want and what they will find interesting. What we are going to turn our attention to next is:

- what you've got to offer
- to what extent what you've got to offer and what the employer is looking for match up.

These matches, where they occur, are what we will be referring to as **strong points**. These strong points are what we need to come across when the employer submits your cover letter to the 'one quick read' test.

Strong points could include any of the following:

- You hold the right qualifications.
- You have the right kind of experience.
- You have received a particular type of training.
- You have the kind of personal qualities the employer is seeking.
- You live in the right place (you won't need relocating).

Remember

A reminder again that strong points mean strong points relating to the job for which you are applying and not what you may see as your strong points generally. For example, you may have a lot of experience in designing applications for a particular brand of computer software but this won't cut much ice with an employer who uses completely different systems. And when it comes to determining what employers will find interesting don't fall into the trap of substituting your own ideas for theirs.

Review your strong points

Now draw up a list of what you consider to be your strong points vis-à-vis the job application you're making and then count up how many you've got. Are there more than six? If there are then go through the list again to make sure they really are strong points. Be ruthless here. Don't let irrelevant information get in the way of the message you want your cover letter to deliver.

Keep the message clear and concise

If the job calls for a mechanical engineering degree and you happen to have one then here we have a strong point. Likewise, if the job calls for someone with experience of designing plastic injection mould tools and you've spent ten years in the trade then here we have another strong point. Simple though it sounds, all you have to do in your cover letter is list these strong points using no more than a few simple sentences to describe each. Break your strong points into paragraphs with a line space between each (bullet points are a good way of doing this).

What you have got now is the core part of your cover letter – one which is relevant and consistent with what the employer is seeking to find. The scene is now set for the employer to find out more by reading your CV. A case of job done? Well, almost.

Use their words

In a world of jargon and buzz words you frequently find employers using terminology which would not necessarily be the same terminology you would use. A tip here is to use the employer's terminology rather than your own to prevent any confusion arising.

Credibility and consistency

We frequently point out to people the importance of consistency in any documents they forward to employers. Why is this?

It is unfortunate, perhaps, but we live in a world where there are people who are prepared to bend the truth a little when they see some advantage for themselves. This bending of the truth often manifests itself in false claims of one kind or another, e.g. false accident claims. As a consequence, employers are on high alert especially when it comes to offering a job to someone. Anything in a cover letter or a CV or on an application form which doesn't ring true is therefore usually enough to ensure the application goes no further. The applicant, of course, is none the wiser.

A common way in which job applicants undermine their credibility is by allowing inconsistencies to creep into the information they present to employers. An example of an inconsistency is where different dates appear against jobs the applicant has held previously. One set of starting and leaving dates appears in the applicant's CV and a completely different set of dates appears in the same person's application form. The same goes for cover letters, where time spent in certain spheres of work may be at variance with what the applicant has said elsewhere. The explanation for these inconsistencies is usually carelessness but the impression that could form in some employers' minds is that they are having the wool pulled over their eyes.

> ### Key point
> Be careful that anything you put in a cover letter is consistent with what appears in your CV. Employers can and do compare the two.

What is a key achievement?

We mention this here because:

- Key achievements and strong points often get mixed up.
- As a result, information gets included in cover letters which shouldn't be there.

Ask someone what they view as their key achievements and they might, for example, mention the fact that last year they raised a large sum of money for famine relief charities by competing in a number of marathons. An achievement, yes, but is it a strong point? The probable answer here is 'no, it isn't' unless of course our marathon runner happened to be applying for a job with a company which has recently taken a high-profile stance in promoting third world agriculture.

What this illustrates is how easy it is to start introducing your own agendas into cover letters and, again, letting irrelevant information get in the way of the message. It may be great you won first prize in a creative writing competition but, if you're applying for a job as an Internal Audit Manager with a firm of grocery wholesalers, it won't do a lot to promote your chances. By all means give achievements such as these a mention at the appropriate point in your CV because what you do with your life says a lot about you generally. But don't clutter your cover letters with information which isn't relevant.

Where you're coming from and what you're seeking to achieve

Employers will want to know why you're applying for a job with them. Central to their thinking will be the avoidance of mismatches. For example, if you're looking for advancement and the job is a downward step then there would be little point in taking your application any further. If, on the other hand, you're at risk of redundancy then it would be a different matter. Making your motives clear is therefore important.

> ## Key point
> Bringing you in for an interview and then finding there is a mismatch between what you are looking for and what the employer has to offer is a waste of everyone's time. The employer's time is wasted and, in your case, you may have taken time off work to go to the interview and/or booked a day's holiday. What this illustrates is that avoiding these mismatches is in everyone's best interests. Often the blame is the applicant's cover letter, which didn't make it clear where the applicant was coming from and what he/she was seeking to achieve.

So, if you're making the application because you feel you're ready for the next step up the ladder, then say so. If on the other hand, you're seeking to branch out into a different field, then, in the same way, make it clear. All it takes in most cases is two sentences tagged onto the first paragraph of your cover letter and a mention in what you have to say about yourself in your CV. Don't leave employers to guess at what's driving you.

Employer friendliness

All of which brings us neatly onto the subject of employer friendliness.

Employer friendliness is important at any stage in a job application and nowhere more so than in the design of a cover letter.

Conciseness and why it's important

Most of what we have done up to now is to do with ensuring that what goes in your cover letter is **relevant**, i.e. it falls in with what employers will be looking to see and will find interesting. Of equal importance, however, is keeping your cover letter **concise**. Why? If you go back to what we said earlier today about the one quick read test, we drew your attention to the fact that cover letters are not always read from start to finish. If readers see nothing that interests them in the first few sentences, they switch off and go no further. OK, it doesn't seem very polite when you've gone to a lot of trouble to prepare the cover letter (and the CV that goes with it) but what you've got to remember is that your cover letter could be the sixtieth the employer has read that day, so anything that doesn't grab the attention straight away could finish up on the reject pile for that reason alone.

Careers advisors usually flag up the need to keep cover letters to one side of A4. The idea here is that one side of A4 will act as a constraint on writers of cover letters so they don't end up producing acres of script which employers will have to plough through. In many cases, employers won't bother.

Conciseness and relevance go together

Please remember this. A cover letter which conforms to the rule of one side of A4 maximum won't do much for you if it doesn't say anything relevant to the job for which you are applying. Similarly, a cover letter which is relevant but which rambles on for page after page won't do the trick for you either.

SUNDAY

MONDAY

TUESDAY

WEDNESDAY

THURSDAY

FRIDAY

SATURDAY

Help employers understand you

Put yourself in the shoes of an employer faced with the job of wading though a pile of job applications and it will help you see how important it is to engage with them quickly, concisely and in a way which will interest them. See the task they face and help them achieve it.

Conclusion

Today we have been looking at what it takes to make a cover letter work for you in a world where in many cases employers are faced with large numbers of applicants competing against one another for a place on the interview list. We have seen the importance of tailoring your cover letters to the jobs for which you are applying and how different attributes you possess will strike different chords with different employers (they are not all the same). We have taught you to pick out which of your attributes make a direct hit with the requirements of the job which interests you and to treat these matches as your strong points – points which will give your cover letter the capacity to attract the attention of readers. At the same time we have looked at employer friendliness and the importance of conciseness, simplicity and making sure your letter is a quick and easy read.

A common complaint you hear from employers is how little effort many applicants make to match their skills, experience and qualifications to the requirements of the job. The ones that do make the effort stand out.

SUNDAY
MONDAY
TUESDAY
WEDNESDAY
THURSDAY
FRIDAY
SATURDAY

Fact-check (answers at the back)

1. Why is it important to keep your cover letters short?
   a) It is the best way of making sure you don't make any spelling mistakes ❑
   b) They will be quick and easy to read ❑
   c) They take less paper and printer ink ❑
   d) They don't detract from your CV ❑

2. What is a strong point?
   a) Something the employer wants and which you have to offer ❑
   b) Where you have better qualifications than those stipulated in the advertisement for the job ❑
   c) Areas in which you have excelled in the past ❑
   d) An outstanding achievement ❑

3. What is the best way of making sure your cover letter will be read?
   a) Typing it neatly ❑
   b) Using a larger than normal font size ❑
   c) Making it interesting and concise ❑
   d) Putting it in an envelope marked 'Urgent' ❑

4. What is the best way of ensuring a cover letter fits onto a single sheet of A4?
   a) Keeping it relevant ❑
   b) Reducing the font size ❑
   c) Cutting out paragraph breaks ❑
   d) Reducing the margins at either side of the page ❑

5. Why is consistency so important?
   a) It shows you pay attention to detail ❑
   b) It prevents confusion ❑
   c) It saves unnecessary questions at interviews ❑
   d) Lack of it will undermine your credibility ❑

6. When is a key achievement a strong point?
   a) When it is relevant to the job for which you are applying ❑
   b) When it receives attention in the media ❑
   c) When it was mentioned at your last appraisal ❑
   d) The two terms have the same meaning ❑

7. Why is it important to tell employers what you're seeking to achieve by moving jobs?
   a) So they know you're ambitious ❑
   b) To avoid mismatches ❑
   c) To soften them up for discussions about salary ❑
   d) It is nothing to do with them ❑

8. In the design of a cover letter, what is the best way of being employer friendly?
   a) By addressing the person to whom you are writing by their first name ❑
   b) By avoiding formal styles of address altogether ❑
   c) By making sure your letter is a quick, easy and interesting read ❑
   d) By sending it with a stamped, addressed envelope ❑

9. Which would you rank as the most important?
a) Keeping your cover letters concise ❏
b) Keeping your cover letters relevant ❏
c) Both a and b together ❏
d) Something else ❏

10. Why are cover letters not always read from start to finish?
a) The people who read them are too lazy ❏
b) There is nothing in the first few sentences which is interesting ❏
c) They are not important ❏
d) The CV that comes with them takes precedence ❏

TUESDAY

The structure
of your letter

Judging by the questions we are asked, nothing causes people more problems with cover letters than how to set them out. For example, if the ad for a job asks you to send your CV to Gillian Smith do you start your letter with 'Dear Gillian' or 'Dear Gillian Smith' or is neither correct? After all you don't know Gillian Smith, so it would be more appropriate to stick to a formal style of address, but then how do you address her? Is she a Miss, a Mrs or a Ms? If you get it wrong, is she going to be offended, which wouldn't be a good start, would it?

This level of uncertainty about how to write a business letter correctly is perhaps a reminder that the art has declined substantially in recent years. The advent of email and other ways of communicating with people on business matters has had a great impact on letter writing and, sad to say, the impact has not always been good. For example, the days when every school-leaver going into an office job went to the local commercial college and learned the basics of good letter writing have long gone.

Today we are going to look at what makes a good cover letter in terms of its structure and, hopefully, at the same time clear up any areas of doubt in your mind about what's right and what isn't.

SUNDAY MONDAY TUESDAY WEDNESDAY THURSDAY FRIDAY SATURDAY

Making a start

Where you do have a big advantage over letter writers of years ago is in the access you have to modern technology. Today you can compose your cover letter on screen, spell check it, edit it if it's too long, alter it if you change your mind about anything and run off drafts as and when you please. So let's make a start with the modern version of a blank sheet of paper, a new document in whatever word-processing software you happen to use.

Fonts

We talked about fonts on Sunday and advised you to stick to standard fonts used in business letters such as Arial or Times New Roman. Sometimes people get tempted to use fonts which fall outside the mainstream because they think it adds interest or says something about their personality. While we can understand the thinking here, what we would rather you do is add interest by making sure anything you say about yourself is relevant. Strange fonts have a tendency to be seen as the choice of strange people.

Font sizes

With font sizes our advice would again be to stick to the sizes you normally find in business letters (11 and 12 points came out as the favourites in a quick sampling exercise we carried out). As we said earlier, people sometimes reduce the size of their fonts so they can squeeze more onto the page. Don't do this because (a) it looks amateurish and (b) it can make letters and CVs difficult to read (i.e. not employer friendly). If you find you're having problems fitting everything onto one sheet of A4, the likely reason is that you're including information which isn't relevant (more on this later).

Margins

The default settings built into your computer software are fine. Don't change them. Don't see it as yet another way of enabling you to cram more onto the page.

White space

Text that is all crammed up, long paragraphs and paragraphs with no space between them are not inviting to the reader, whereas plenty of white space is naturally pleasing to the eye (employer friendly again). Two spaces after every full stop and a line space between paragraphs not only look professional but also encourage people to read what you have written.

Page heading

Start at the top of the page with your address. Many of you will already have a letter heading set up as a template in the documents on your computer. Most of the ones we have seen are excellent and an example appears at the end of Wednesday's chapter. Again, avoid any temptation to unleash your artistic talents. A cover letter is not the place to do it.

Email and telephone points of contact

These should also be included in your page heading (again, see the example on Wednesday). When employers are happy that you tick the boxes, they might want to invite you in for an interview. Often they will do this by ringing you up or emailing you, so, as part of being employer friendly, you can make it easy for them by having your phone numbers and email address where they don't have to search for them, i.e. in the heading at the top of your cover letter. Your email address and telephone points of contact will also, of course, feature in your CV but information as important as how to get hold of you stands repetition.

The date

A letter which isn't dated is worthless, or so we were always taught. More to the point, a cover letter without a date on it has the mark of one which the writer sends off every time he/she applies for a job. Put the date at the top of the page immediately underneath the letter heading with a line space in between.

Left-hand justification

Some people indent their paragraphs but most writers of business letters don't. There is nothing wrong with indented paragraphs except they look old-fashioned and for this reason are best avoided.

Name and address of the person to whom you are writing

The ad for the job will tell you the name of the person to write to or occasionally you may be invited to send your application to someone who is identified only by their job title, e.g. Chief Executive, Human Resources Manager or Consultant. The simple rule here is to follow the instruction to the letter. So, if you're invited to write to Gillian Smith, write to Gillian Smith. If, on the other hand, you're invited to write to Mrs Gillian Smith then do that. The same goes for letters to the Chief Executive or the Human Resources Manager. In some cases the person you're writing to will have a job title as well as a name, e.g. Gillian Smith, Human Resources Manager. Here again, follow the instruction and include both the name and the job title. Who knows, there may be more than one Gillian Smith in the organization you're writing to and it's important your letter finds its way to the right one!

> # Warning!
>
> We've said it once but we'll say it again. Be very careful when you're typing in people's names and make sure you copy them correctly. The same goes for the names, addresses and postcodes of businesses. Mistakes are more common than you may think and, not surprisingly, the person whose name you've spelt incorrectly will notice it straight away. How they view your failure to get their name right will be very much a matter for them, but, needless to say, the first impression you make won't be good.

Forms of salutation

Back to where we came in at the start of today. When you're asked to send your application to Gillian Smith, how do you address her? 'Dear Gillian' might possibly be seen as a bit familiar but then if you want to avoid this problem you run into another one. Is she Miss, Mrs or Ms? Many people faced with this situation resort to using 'Dear Madam'. OK, so there's nothing wrong with 'Dear Madam' but it's hardly engaging/employer friendly. There is also evidence to suggest that someone addressed by name is more likely to reply to you. Our advice? Start the letter 'Dear Gillian Smith'. It's professional, it's formal without being starchy, yet it's personal and directed at someone in the most fixating way, i.e. by using their name.

   Writing to a man doesn't have the same complications as writing to a woman, so, if you're invited to send your application to John Phillips, you can address him as 'Dear John Phillips' or 'Dear Mr Phillips' – either is acceptable. Given this choice our preference would be for 'Dear John Phillips' because including his first name is more engaging.

But what if you're not given the person's name? What if the ad asks you to write to the Human Resources Manager? Does this mean addressing them as 'Dear Sir' or 'Dear Madam' but, as you don't know whether the Human Resources Manager is a man or a woman does this leave you with no choice other than starting your letter 'Dear Sir or Madam'? Perhaps it does and let's straight away say there's nothing wrong with 'Dear Sir or Madam' except it's not very engaging. One approach you might like to consider is writing to 'Dear Human Resources Manager'. It's a bit different and engages with the person you're writing to more than a starchy 'Dear Sir or Madam' would do. We'll leave it up to you.

Make it clear why you're writing

You're writing because you want to apply for a job so make this clear right away and, at the same time, make it clear which job interests you. We say this for the simple reason that organizations are often advertising more than one position, so confusion can and does arise. The fall-out for you is if your application (your cover letter and CV) ends up on the wrong pile. Unfortunately, in large organizations, where opening the post is often left to someone quite junior, this happens more than people think.

The best way to make your intentions clear is by putting a heading in bold at the top of your letter identifying the job for which you're applying. For example:

Re: Production Manager (ref: XX/999)

Not all employers will ask you to quote a reference but, if they do, put it in the heading where it will stand out (as in the example).

Your opening paragraph

In your opening paragraph:

● **Tell the employer where you saw the job advertised.**
  Recruitment advertising is an expensive item and employers like to know which publications/websites yield

the best results. Feedback from applicants is therefore
important to them and, from your point of view, it is all
part of being employer friendly.

- **Explain why you're applying for the job.** This goes back
to what we had to say yesterday about making it plain
(a) where you're coming from and (b) what you're seeking
to achieve.

SUNDAY MONDAY TUESDAY WEDNESDAY THURSDAY FRIDAY SATURDAY

Example of an opening paragraph

I wish to apply for the position advertised in last
night's *Evening Bugle*. I am currently employed as
a Production Manager in the automotive components
industry and I am seeking a new position because
the plant where I am based is scheduled for
closure in six months' time.

Your killer bullet points

Your killer bullet points are the strong points we looked at
yesterday: the matches between what employers want and
what you've got to offer – in other words, how you fit the job
specification.

Registering your strong points doesn't call for anything
elaborate. Two or three short sentences are usually
sufficient – enough to whet the reader's appetite and focus
his/her interest.

Warning!

Intent on catching the reader's eye with what they
consider to be their most winning features, some people
resort to using capital (upper-case) letters, underlining or
picking out key words in red. Don't do this because (a) it
is not necessary and (b) it's the written word's equivalent
of shouting, i.e. not very polite.

The example cover letter in Wednesday's chapter shows how to list your strong points.

Closing paragraph

All you have to do now is to tell the employer your CV is attached. At the same time say a few words about your availability, by which we mean:

● your availability to attend interviews
● your availability to start a new job.

> **Example of a closing paragraph**
>
> A copy of my CV is attached. I am available to attend an interview at any time except between [ ] and [ ] when I am overseas on a business trip. My current employment is subject to four weeks' notice.

Availability

With availability here are a few dos and don'ts to consider.

Don't say you're only available for interviews after 6.00 p.m. or on Saturday mornings. If you do, you won't find too many takers.

Do try to give employers as much leeway as you can with interview times.

Don't say you're available when you're not.

Do give details of any holidays, dates when you can't attend etc.

Don't leave unanswered questions. For example if your branch is closing in six months' time, does it mean you can't start a job for six months?

Do see it from the employer's point of view. If you are on a redundancy list and the date you've been given is still some way off, tell the employer what the position would be if they offered you a job. For example, are there any arrangements for early release?

Don't (if you're employed) make statements such as 'I could start a new job at any time', which gives the impression you would leave your current position without giving the proper notice. Understandably, employers don't warm to people who are prepared to act in this way; it's a bad first impression.

Do state the period of notice set out in your terms of employment.

Signing off

All that remains now is to finish your letter by signing off in the proper way.

There are only two acceptable ways of ending a business letter: one is 'Yours sincerely;' and the other is 'Yours faithfully'. So forget 'best wishes' or 'kind regards' or anything else you may put at the end of a letter written to someone you have had correspondence with before.

'Yours sincerely' or 'Yours faithfully'

The rules here are simple. If your letter starts with a name (e.g. Gillian Smith) then you end it 'Yours sincerely'. If it starts 'Dear Sir' or 'Dear Madam' then the more formal 'Yours faithfully' is correct.

Sign your name

Leave five line spaces for your signature and then type in your name (first name and surname). Initials (e.g. J. Brown or, worse still, Miss J. Brown) look standoffish and old-fashioned when the general idea is to engage with the person you're writing to.

> ### **Warning!**
>
> If your letter is a hard copy that's going to go in the post, don't forget to sign it.
>
> Though the reason is usually oversight, letters that haven't been signed have unfortunate connotations for employers. Rather like application forms which come back without being signed, the omission could suggest the information you've given in your letter isn't true.

Anything else?

Insert another line space after your name and then type in: Attached CV

This is another way of bringing your cover letter and CV together.

Footnote: staple your cover letter and CV together to minimize the risk of them being separated when they arrive at the other end.

Envelopes

On Sunday we drew your attention to using a full-size white A4 envelope so your cover letter and CV don't have to be folded. Typing the employer's name and address on an envelope can pose a challenge and, even with the best of us, it can result in a few failed attempts! You can of course print off a sheet of labels in anticipation of having further correspondence with the employer. However, don't worry about hand-writing an envelope provided you do it neatly. In any case, envelopes are usually discarded once they are opened.

Mailing cover letters

The reliability of postal services is usually a question of where you live. However, to avoid any risk of your job application being delayed in the post (and arriving too late), it's well worth investing in whatever guaranteed next-day delivery service is available in your part of the world.

Emails

Some job advertisements ask you to submit your application by email. Email scores highly in terms of speed and certainty of getting there. If the email is addressed to a named individual it is also a safe bet that he/she will open it and read it straight away.

The normal way of submitting an application by email is to put your cover letter in the body of the email and your CV in a file attachment. Any problem with this? Yes: what can happen is the email and the file attachment get separated – the usual reason being the file attachment gets printed off and the email doesn't. So all the effort you've put into preparing your cover letter is wasted. To avoid this we suggest you do as follows. Put a copy of your cover letter (complete with your name, address, points of contact etc. at the top) in the file attachment with your CV. Effectively your cover letter becomes the first page of your CV and you will have done your best to ensure it is assembled in this way when it comes off the printer at the other end.

Keeping control

Keeping your cover letter and CV together in this way is an example of **keeping control**; those of you who have read our other books in the In A Week series will be familiar with this principle already. In the context of job applications, keeping control means keeping your hand on the steering wheel as far as you can, so your applications go in directions which you want them to go in. In this case you will have kept control over what finishes up on the desk of whoever will be making the decision on what happens to your application next.

Warning!

The issue of not being able to open files attached to emails is a serious one. People who process job applications won't as a rule be IT experts, so an email attachment which won't open stands a reasonable chance of remaining unopened. Rather than leave this to chance we suggest you send a test email with a file attachment either to your work email address or to one of your friends or family.

Writing style and good English

We have had a lot to say already about how candidates let themselves down with spelling mistakes and bad grammar. Email has brought a new dimension to this problem with some people feeling that it's acceptable to allow lapses to creep in when corresponding with someone by email. The first point to make, therefore, is that it isn't acceptable and just as much care needs to be taken. Email also, for some reason, encourages people to adopt a more relaxed (casual) style of prose. Here is where 'Hi' and 'Cheers' are sometimes used in place of more conventional forms of salutation and signing off.

As a job application progresses, you will hopefully receive emails from the employer inviting you to interviews and second interviews, and, who knows, an email offering you the job. Here you may find the employer starts off with 'Hi' and ends up 'Regards' or 'Best wishes', which is on the whole a good sign of someone seeking to engage with you. Where this happens it is perfectly acceptable for you to respond in the same way; indeed to do otherwise might be seen as unfriendly or standoffish.

Bad English, as we have said several times, is usually the result of carelessness and, as such, it can be corrected by paying more care and attention to what you write. A tip you may find useful is to avoid some of the more obvious grammatical clangers by keeping your sentences short. Wandering off into subordinate clauses invites trouble but even more of a problem, we find, is that the meaning starts to become obscure. Take it from us, readers of cover letters won't spend time racking their brains over whether you meant this or that or something completely different altogether.

Note

We'll be coming back to writing style and good English on Saturday.

Conclusion

You may already be well versed in the art of writing good business letters, so a lot of what we have looked at today may be going over old ground. There is, however, usually room for improvement and at the end of the day, practice makes perfect. The more cover letters you write, the better you become at it.

Today what we hope to have shown you is that, if you do it right, setting out a good cover letter, isn't difficult and will score you points on the favourable first impressions front.

Also today we have looked at the challenge you face when you are asked to submit an application by email. It looks straightforward enough but unfortunately there is more scope for something going wrong; hence the few words about the importance of doing the best you can to keep control.

You have now arrived at the point where you are ready to put what you have learned over the last three days into practice. Tomorrow we will start by looking at how to put together a cover letter for attacking the visible or advertised job market.

Fact-check (answers at the back)

1. When is it correct to start a cover letter with 'Hi'?
   a) When you're sending it by email ☐
   b) When you're writing to a named person ☐
   c) If you're under 25 ☐
   d) Never ☐

2. How is it best to end a letter which starts 'Dear Gillian Smith'?
   a) Yours faithfully ☐
   b) Yours sincerely ☐
   c) Best wishes ☐
   d) Yours truly ☐

3. Where on a cover letter do you put the date?
   a) Under your address at the top ☐
   b) At the end ☐
   c) It doesn't matter where you put it ☐
   d) Under the address of the person to whom you're writing ☐

4. Why is it important to identify the job for which you're applying?
   a) It helps to show you're interested ☐
   b) It is a way of making sure your letter is read ☐
   c) It is a way of making a good first impression ☐
   d) The employer may be advertising more than one position ☐

5. Why is it bad practice to pick out key points in your letter with capital (upper-case) letters?
   a) It's not necessary ☐
   b) It doesn't create a good first impression ☐
   c) It is the written equivalent of shouting ☐
   d) All three of the above ☐

6. What's wrong with not signing your letter?
   a) Nothing is wrong with it ☐
   b) To some employers it might suggest you're not telling the truth ☐
   c) It could show you don't own a decent pen ☐
   d) Employers need to see evidence of your handwriting ☐

7. In an email, where is the best place to put a cover letter?
   a) In the body of the email ☐
   b) With your CV in a file attachment ☐
   c) In both a and b ☐
   d) In a separate file attachment ☐

8. What is the most common cause of spelling mistakes?
   a) Bad teaching in schools ☐
   b) Spellcheckers ☐
   c) Carelessness and not checking ☐
   d) Tiredness ☐

9. Why is it a good idea to keep sentences short?
a) There is less scope for grammatical errors ❏
b) It takes less effort ❏
c) Their meaning is usually clear ❏
d) They don't need to be checked ❏

10. How do you choose between sending in an application by email and putting it in the post?
a) It depends on whether you've got the employer's email address or not ❏
b) You don't. You do what the advertisement tells you to do ❏
c) You send it by email if you want your application to get there quicker ❏
d) Flip a coin ❏

WEDNESDAY

Attacking the visible market

Today we're going to look at what to some people is the toughest challenge of all: designing a cover letter to attack the visible or advertised job market, where the issues will be engaging with and overcoming competition.

How many applications are received for a job will depend to a large extent on:

● How good is the job?
● How widely has it been advertised?

It goes almost without saying that a good job which has been given prominent advertising will attract large numbers of applicants. In recessionary times, these numbers increase several-fold, reflecting the fact that:

● good opportunities are thin on the ground
● more people are chasing them.

What this means from the employer's point of view, of course, is that every time they advertise a position they are faced with excessive numbers of people who are capable of doing it. The issue for the applicant therefore becomes one of how on earth are they going to make themselves stand out from the crowd?

Against this backdrop the job of a cover letter takes on bigger proportions. It has to perform feats out of the ordinary, which sets the scene nicely for today's lesson.

Be aware of what you're up against

Applicants for jobs usually have the disadvantage of not knowing what competition they're up against, in terms of both its quantity and its quality. In some cases they proceed blithely, hardly moving out of first gear, in the vain hope that the cover letter and CV they're used to churning out will be good enough. When the reply comes back saying they've not got on the interview list, they don't understand. As they see it, they've got all the qualifications needed to do the job – indeed they could do it with their eyes shut – so why haven't they been given the chance to go further? Usually people in this position blame the employer for not reading their cover letter and CV properly. What they rarely see is that the responsibility for not getting their message across rests squarely on them.

Checklist

We have prepared a checklist for you which should help to highlight where you may be going wrong with the cover letters you're submitting. At the same time the checklist will act as a revision exercise by picking out the main points from lessons so far this week.

Go through the checklist and put a tick against the questions to which you can truthfully answer 'yes'.

- Are your cover letters typed on one sheet of plain white A4 paper?
- Do you design a new cover letter every time you apply for a job?
- Are they set out in the way we described in yesterday's lesson?
- Other than using a spellchecker, do you check your spelling and grammar rigorously?
- Are you identifying your strong points?
- Are your strong points matched to the skills, experience and qualifications the employer is seeking?

- Is everything in your cover letters capable of being understood in one quick read?
- Do you check for consistency between the information in your cover letters and what appears in your CV?
- Do you always remember to sign your cover letters?
- Have you done background research into employers and taken the trouble to find out more about them?
- Are you getting your applications in the post promptly?
- With emails, are you including a copy of your cover letter in the file attachment with your CV?
- Are you making it clear to employers what interests you about working for them?

Defining the task you face

In every trawl of applicants for jobs which have been advertised, there are usually a few no-hopers, people who are not properly qualified to do the job but who thought they'd give it a shot anyway. However, take these no-hopers out and what employers usually find they are left with is a large number of people who, on paper at least, seem be quite capable of doing the job.

Most people these days are quite savvy when it comes to applying for jobs. They read books such as this one, they go on the Internet, and by and large they know what to do. So the task you face is a tough one. Somehow you've got to stand out from a crowd of people who in many cases will be every bit as good as you.

How employers see it

Employers faced with large numbers of applicants can afford to be picky and choosy when it comes to deciding whom to interview. On the one hand they won't want to miss the best applicant but on the other hand they are constrained by time so they won't be able to see everyone. What follows, therefore, is a whittling down of candidates done on the basis of who, on paper, matches the specification closest. Out at this stage go people with a question mark over what they have to offer – for example, people who haven't made themselves very clear in their cover letters and CVs. Phoning people up and asking them 'Did you mean this or that?' doesn't figure at all in this process.

> ## Key point
>
> In these highly competitive situations 'once' really does mean 'once' when it comes to counting how many times your cover letter will be read. It has to register with employers first time because it won't get another chance.

Who stands out?

What the decisions tend to rest on at this crucial stage is 'who stands out?' So back to the strong points which you've listed out in your cover letter. How do they measure up and, more importantly, how do they measure up when other people also have strong points to offer? Is it a case of whose strong points are strongest? Well, perhaps it is, but where we need to start with this is by asking two questions:

● How have you described your strong points?
● Have you undersold them?

What's different about you?

Let's take an example:
   You are applying for a senior management job with an Italian-owned business where one of the main requirements

is that you speak Italian. OK, you do speak Italian, but what's a safe bet here is that most of the other candidates can also speak Italian or they wouldn't have applied for the job in the first place. However, what's different about you is the fact that one of your parents is Italian so to you Italian is practically a first language. What's the betting no one else can say the same? So here potentially you have something which will make you stand out from the crowd. All you have to do now is mention it and what better place than in your cover letter?

Warning

When you have something special to say about yourself there is a fine line between telling it the way it is and overstating the case. Self-eulogies of the sort we've all seen in cover letters and CVs don't go down well with employers, mainly because they've heard it all before. What is intended to make them sit up and take notice in fact makes them switch off and yawn.

Your unique selling points

What we're looking at here are your unique selling points or USPs. In a nutshell your USPs are:

- what mark you out as different from the rest
- what you need to bring out if you are going to be successful at engaging with and overcoming competition.

Why you want the job

How else can you make yourself stand out from the crowd? In your cover letter is there anything which will make employers warm to you where they may not warm to others?

Let's take another example:

Two people, Jack and Jill, both with more or less the same qualifications, apply for a job.

In his cover letter Jack says he is making the application because he is at risk of redundancy.

Jill, on the other hand, tells the employer she wants the job because she has read about what the company does and wants to be part of it.

In Jack's case, the impression he is creating is that he is in a tight corner and any job will do to get him out of it. The further impression is that he only applied for the job because of the situation he is in and not because of any great interest in it.

With Jill, she is telling the employer she wants to come and work for them and why. The message in this case is one the employer wants to hear.

OK, we may feel sorry for Jack because his situation is all too familiar to us – but what the example is intended to show is how statements like 'I'm looking for a job because I'm being made redundant in six months' time' don't make much of an impression when an employer has lots of other applicants knocking on the door – applicants who may be like Jill.

The message? Have something **positive** to say about why you're applying for a job – for example, say you want to come and work for the business because of its excellent reputation or because the position you've seen advertised fits in exactly with where you see your next move (or both).

Give the employer something to get excited about, which you will only do if you feel excited about it too.

Say it with flair and conviction

This leads us to where a lot of cover letters fall down. The messages in them are flat. The words are just words and, take it from us, reading one cover letter after another can be a mind-numbing experience. Then thankfully one comes along which is lively and engaging and it stands out like a splash of colour against a grey background.

Writing is a craft, and learning to write in a way which will make readers' eyes light up isn't a gift which comes overnight. However, there is a lot we can all do to make what we write more engaging. Just as an experiment, what we would like you to do is to take an example of something you want to say about yourself and, giving it your best shot, write it in four different ways. Then in a few days' time go back to what you've written and see what you think or ask someone you know to give you an opinion. Hopefully what this experience will prove to you is that you can always better what you did first time, remembering that better in this context means better from the standpoint of making what you've written have a bigger impact on the reader. Though we're not expecting you to aspire to the standards of the world's great literary figures (at least not yet!) you can do wonders and even surprise yourself with a bit of effort and inclination. Most of all, see the job of engaging with your readers as important and something worth doing, something which will help to make you stand out.

Write the way you speak

A good way to approach the job of writing a cover letter is to imagine you're having a conversation with a work colleague. Use words which come naturally to you and keep the tone businesslike yet at the same time friendly.

Writing in this way can take a bit of getting used to but it will come with practice.

Conviction

Delivering your messages in ways which readers find easy to follow and understand has the added advantage of making them authoritative and more convincing. For the proof, try reading a newspaper article written by a good journalist and see how many times you find yourself nodding along in agreement.

Making it interesting

If there is anything interesting about any of the experience you've had, then, provided it's relevant to the job, say so. Picking out points of interest like this is a way of making employers want to find out more about you by looking at your CV. If, for example, you've worked for a business in the past which has many of the same customers as the employer you're writing to now, then make sure to mention it.

Key point

A point to bear in mind here is that in many larger organizations your application will go to someone who may not be completely familiar with what it is that you do; for example, a human resources manager or a consultant who has been brought in to handle the recruitment exercise up to first interview stage. Thus, the fact you spent five years in a customer-facing role with one of the employer's biggest competitors may not register unless you point it out. Your experience makes you a red-hot candidate for the job but, if someone isn't familiar with the names of all the players in the industry, the point may escape them.

What makes success?

Attacking the visible market is by its very nature difficult. Even if you do everything right the odds are still heavily stacked against you. For example, where there are 200 applicants for a job and only 12 are called in for interview, your chances of being one of the lucky ones are slim, to say the least.

Why are we saying this? For the simple reason that getting a letter advising you that you've not been selected to attend an interview can be a big setback, especially when you've built your hopes up. Not perhaps appreciating the scale of the task you faced in the first place, your thoughts immediately turn to where you may have gone wrong. Sooner or later the finger starts to point in the direction of your cover letter and CV. Your cover letter and CV were designed, after all, to get you interviews, so their failure to do so is automatically seen as a bad reflection on their effectiveness.

Although some kind of inquest into why your job applications don't appear to be enjoying much success makes good sense, it equally makes good sense not to leap immediately to the conclusion that your cover letters and CVs aren't working for you. Success on the visible job market is often more to do with the ability to keep going in the face of what seems like adversity. Tinkering with the finer points of cover letters is in many cases wasted effort which would be much better put into getting off the next job application.

> If you want to know more about why job applications don't turn into interviews, try reading another of our books in this series: *Job Hunting In A Week*.

Example of a cover letter for attacking the visible market

John Everyman has seen a position for a Factory Manager advertised in the local evening newspaper. The position is with a business which is part of a large multi-national and which makes aluminium extruded sections for the construction industry.

John Everyman
12 Acacia Gardens
Anytown AT99 9XX
Tel: xxx xxxxx
Mobile: xxx xxxxxxx
email – Johne@xxx.com

29 March 2013

Julie Robertson
Human Resources Manager
XX Extruded Sections Limited
PO Box xx
Anytown
AT11 1ZZ

Dear Julie Robertson

Re: Factory Manager

I wish to apply for the position advertised in last night's *Evening Bugle*. You will see from my CV (attached) that I am currently employed as a Cell Manager in a precision engineering company where I am responsible for 120 operatives working four on/four off continental shifts. I am aware of XX Extruded Sections' excellent reputation and I would welcome the opportunity to talk further about joining your management team.

With regard to the requirements set out in your advertisement:

Modern manufacturing techniques Information on the training I have received is given in my CV. In my present job I have been closely involved with the introduction of fast tooling changes.

Qualifications I have a degree in mechanical engineering

Management experience I have been in my present position for five years and previously worked for eight years as Shift Manager in charge of a high volume production unit.

Additional information For five years post apprenticeship I worked on the design of a range of dies and tools including plastic and aluminium extrusion dies.

Apart from Monday morning when I chair production meetings I am available for interview at any time. My current employment is subject to one calendar month's notice.

I look forward to hearing from you.

Yours sincerely

John Everyman

Attached: CV

Key points to pick out from John Everyman's cover letter are as follows:

- It looks professional.
- It is well written.
- It makes a good first impression.
- It is a quick and easy read.
- Everything in it is relevant to the job for which he is applying.
- He has told the employer what makes him a serious contender for the job.
- He has done some background research into XX Extruded Sections and found out they too operate four on/four off continental shifts.
- He figured correctly that mentioning his experience of managing four on/four off shifts would work in his favour.
- He also figured that other applicants may not have the same experience or, if they did, they may not mention it.
- The mention of fast tooling changes is neat. He has figured that non-productive time spent on changing dies and how to reduce it must figure prominently in XX's thinking.
- He has worked out his experience in designing aluminium extrusion dies is another unique selling point. He sees it as

a safe bet that not many people applying for the job (if any) would have experience of both production management and the design of dies.

- The mention of chairing production meetings on Monday morning is a nice touch. It shows his loyalty to his employer and that the discharge of his duties comes first.

Conclusion

Today we have looked at the challenging task of designing a cover letter to attack the visible market, where it's not just what you have to offer that you have to consider but what other applicants have to offer as well. We have directed your attention to the following:

● What makes you different from the rest? What are your unique selling points and how do you get them across?

● What do employers want to hear you saying? Why do people who are passionate about wanting the job stand out?

● Is there anything interesting in your background (anything that would make the reader of your cover letter sit up and single you out)?

Finally, today we looked at how to condition your expectations when you're applying for jobs on the visible market. You won't get an interview every time and to think otherwise is not being realistic. If, on the other hand, you are getting some interviews and the jobs are good jobs then it is probably a sign your cover letters and CVs are working.

SUNDAY
MONDAY
TUESDAY
WEDNESDAY
THURSDAY
FRIDAY
SATURDAY

Fact-check (answers at the back)

1. What is the visible job market?
   a) Jobs in the public sector ❏
   b) Jobs which have been advertised ❏
   c) Jobs in high-profile industries ❏
   d) Jobs which are only open to graduates ❏

2. What's the main job your cover letters have to do when you're applying for jobs on the visible market?
   a) Engage with and overcome competition ❏
   b) Cover up your defects ❏
   c) Make employers take you seriously ❏
   d) Draw attention to your qualifications ❏

3. In the context of job applications, what is a unique selling point?
   a) Where there is a match between the requirements of the job and what you have to offer ❏
   b) A point in your favour ❏
   c) An unusual requirement in a job specification ❏
   d) Where you have something to offer which none of the others do ❏

4. What's important about unique selling points?
   a) They make you look better than you are ❏
   b) They make you stand out from the rest ❏
   c) Employers are fooled by them ❏
   d) They make it easier for you to negotiate a better salary than the one advertised ❏

5. What's wrong with giving impending redundancy as your reason for applying for a job?
   a) Unscrupulous employers may see it as an opportunity to negotiate a lower salary with you ❏
   b) Employers don't want people who've been picked out for redundancy ❏
   c) It's not a good enough reason for wanting the job ❏
   d) There's nothing wrong with it ❏

6. In competitive job situations, which of the following will help you most with getting interviews?
   a) Telling employers you're the greatest ❏
   b) Sending in a cover letter printed on red paper ❏
   c) Provided it's relevant to the job, highlighting areas where you may have more to offer than other applicants ❏
   d) Telling employers about your sporting achievements ❏

7. What's good about cover letters that are well written?
   a) They stand out ❏
   b) They make you look clever ❏
   c) They make you look more assertive ❏
   d) They show you're serious ❏

8. What do you need to take into account when you send a cover letter to a 'generalist' such as a consultant or a human resources manager?

a) They'll be more fussy about bad grammar and spelling mistakes ❏

b) They may not be familiar with what you do or the terminology you use ❏

c) They take a long time to answer ❏

d) They are more likely to read the letter than someone who is busy ❏

9. When do you need to think about designing a new cover letter?

a) When you're not getting interviews ❏

b) When you're only getting interviews occasionally ❏

c) When the interviews you're getting are for jobs which don't interest you ❏

d) Every time you apply for a job ❏

10. When is it better to send a cover letter by email?

a) When it's hard to get to the post ❏

b) When you know there will be large numbers of applicants for the job ❏

c) When you're on the last minute to get it off quickly ❏

d) Only when the advertisement for the job invites you to use email ❏

THURSDAY

Attacking the invisible market

Today we are going to look at designing a cover letter for attacking the invisible job market:

- jobs which aren't advertised
- jobs which for one reason or another employers keep to themselves.

There is no way of accurately measuring the size of the invisible job market but it's fair to say that it is:

- big
- bigger than most people think.

One way of accessing the invisible job market is by sending out speculative mail shots either by post or in email form. Designing a cover letter for this purpose is what we will be looking at today. The rules – as we shall see – are very different from the rules for attacking the visible market. Notably there is no job advertisement to look at:

- nothing to tell you what the employer views as important
- nothing to give you clues on how to prioritize your key skills and achievements.

What you want a speculative mail shot to achieve

The hope with a speculative mail shot is that your application ends up on the right desk at the right time.

- **Right desk** means the desk of whoever is responsible for hiring people like you.
- **Right time** means when there is a need to recruit or a need to recruit is about to arise.

Failing this, what you want to achieve with your speculative mail shot is to ensure your cover letter and CV are put away in the **right file**. The **right file** in this case means the file the employer revisits when the need to recruit next comes up.

Revisiting previous applicants

Employers faced with a vacancy to fill often start by looking back at the details of interesting candidates they've kept on file. If they come across someone suitable then:

- The 'someone suitable' is asked in for an interview.
- If he/she ticks the boxes, he/she gets offered the job.
- No one else gets a look in.

What opportunities are you seeking to source?

A further point to consider here is that your speculative mail shot could connect with a vacancy which has already been advertised (one you've missed). In other words, the employer is already recruiting, so your application is added to the list. However, the idea behind a speculative mail shot is not to source jobs which are already out in the market place but to prise out two types of opportunity:

- **first**, where the employer is thinking about recruiting but hasn't got round to it yet

- **second**, where your letter and CV generates sufficient interest to get an employer thinking 'Can we create a slot for this person?'

We would add a third situation here which is typical of recruitment in recessionary times. Employers faced with a gap in their ranks hold fire and wait for signs of recovery to show before they commit themselves to hiring. An enquiry from someone who looks interesting can often tip the balance in these situations.

The task your cover letter has to perform

Employers are bombarded with unsolicited job applications and most of them are seen as time-wasters. Therefore – rather like applications for jobs which have been advertised – the first feat your cover letter has to perform is to make your application stand out from the rest. This is not easy when, as we said a little earlier, you start off with little idea of what qualities the employer sees as important. You are left fishing in the dark – or so it seems.

Tap into your professional network

Before sending in an unsolicited job application a question you need to ask yourself is 'Why is this employer going to be interested in me?'

Apart from seeing what's useful in the way of information out there on the Internet, a good place to start is with your professional network, the circle of contacts you have built up over the years. For example:

- Do you know anyone who works for the employer or who has worked for them in the past? If so, what can they tell you?
- Do you know anyone who has business links with the employer – for example a supplier?
- Do you know any of the employer's competitors?

The value of background research

Often it's just a case of making a few phone calls and, although at the end of it you may not have a complete picture, you will have more information than you started off with and hopefully enough to know what is going to interest the employer and what isn't.

Example: a few years ago we talked to a design engineer who was looking for a new job. Before she sent off a speculative letter, she found out from a contact in the industry what computer-aided design package the employer used. She then gave her experience of working with the package a prominent place in her cover letter and a few days later she got a phone call to ask her to attend an interview. Making the match, getting across a strong point, worked for her.

Intelligent guesswork

There is nothing wrong with intelligent guesswork, particularly in situations where the information available to you would otherwise be thin on the ground. Yesterday in the example of John Everyman we saw how he guessed his knowledge of fast tooling changes would add weight to his application to XX Extruded Sections.

Whom to write to

The next question you face when you sit down to the job of writing a speculative cover letter is whom do you send it to?

With everything we've said so far about engaging with employers and being employer friendly, it goes against the grain to suggest we get over this problem by writing to the business rather than a named individual, starting the letter with 'Dear Sirs...'

Get a name

It's important with a speculative cover letter that it is sent to the **right** person and, as we noted earlier, right in this context means the person who is responsible for hiring people like you. So, for example, if you're an accountant the right person may be the Finance Director, or, if you're putting yourself forward for a job at the top of the tree, you may need to send it to the Chief Executive.

How do you find out the name of the person you want to write to? This is the easy bit. The names of key job holders are often on websites. Failing this, just phone up and ask.

Warning!

Phoning up and asking has a danger, and it is this. The person you speak to may, for no reason other than being helpful, give you the name of the Human Resources Manager or a personal assistant through whom job applications are normally channelled. Human resources managers and personal assistants don't hire anyone, except perhaps for people looking for jobs in human resources management. Note also that human resources managers have bigger piles of unsolicited letters on their desks than anyone else, whereas people such as finance directors won't be quite so inundated.

Explain your ambitions

Now you have:

- a name
- a list of what you're hoping the person you're writing to is going to find relevant and interesting.

What you need to do next is decide what you want to say about why you're writing to the employer, i.e. what kind of opportunities you are hoping they will have.

> ## Case study
>
> Jenny X, a young and highly successful key account executive with one of the leading names in the food industry, wrote off to a number of competitors with the sole idea of improving her salary. Because of her background and track record she had no difficulty at all when it came to getting interviews but, because she said nothing about her pay ambitions in her cover letter (or her CV), she found the jobs with the competitors were in money terms sideways or in some cases backwards steps. The result? She used up a lot of her holiday entitlement on going to interviews which were effectively a waste of time. The fault? Regrettably it was hers.

A lot of unsolicited letters we have seen are like Jenny X's: strong on what the candidate has to offer but weak/silent/unclear on what they're seeking to achieve. In Jenny X's case, our guess is she fell into the trap of not talking about money because she thought it might make her seem greedy and avaricious. However, what needs to be considered here is that without any information on what's driving candidates – where they're coming from and what they're seeking to achieve – employers won't have a clue. They too are left groping in the dark and this can and does lead to misunderstandings.

SUNDAY
MONDAY
TUESDAY
WEDNESDAY
THURSDAY
FRIDAY
SATURDAY

> ## Key point
>
> With a speculative letter everything is the other way round. It's you, not the employer, who designs the job specification. It's what you want, not what the employer wants. It's what the employer has to offer, not you.

Be open and explicit

Again, this is important, and Jenny X's case will serve as a good example. Money, as we know, is a sensitive subject but in her cover letter she needed to make it clear:

● that she was looking for a better salary
● what she was earning now and the figure she was aspiring to.

By being open and explicit, Jenny X would have saved both the employers and herself a lot of time.

Note: being open doesn't just apply to salary. It is equally important to be open about your other ambitions. For example, if you're looking for an upwards rather than a sideways move in terms of your position on the management ladder then again you need to say so.

Mark your letter and envelope 'confidential'

Here is a tip. If you want your letter and CV to be opened by the person to whom it's addressed and not someone else (e.g. a post room clerk) then the best way to ensure this happens is by marking the letter and the envelope 'confidential'.

Send out unsolicited job applications in small batches

Taking time off work to go to interviews may not be a problem for you if you're in one of these situations:

● you are unemployed
● you are in full-time education

- your employer is happy for you to take time off work, e.g. you're being made redundant and your employer is supporting your efforts to find another job
- your hours of work are flexible
- you work part-time or on shifts so you have free time during the day
- your movements aren't closely supervised.

Otherwise you need to be careful how many speculative job enquiries you send out in one go. If you don't, you can find yourself overwhelmed with requests to attend interviews, leaving you with the problem of having to negotiate time off work (which could be awkward) or (the worst situation) having to turn interviews down.

Key point

Because you don't have any idea how your speculative enquiries are going to be received, it is best to send them out in small batches – say two or three at a time with gaps of a few weeks in between. Another reason for this advice is that the job of putting together a cover letter and CV for a 'cold' mail shot calls for a lot of input in terms of both background research and time spent in front of the screen. Sending out enquiries in small batches will therefore be more manageable for you.

Put it in the post

When you've written your speculative cover letter you have to decide whether to send it in the post or by email. Our advice? Put it in the post. Why do we say this? For the simple reason that emails aren't always printed off. Say, for example, you're looking for a job as a logistics manager and you email your speculative enquiry to the Head of Operations in a large distribution business. The Head of Operations will read your email on screen, possibly with interest, but if there isn't a current vacancy for a logistics manager there is a strong chance he/she will delete it.

If you go back to what we said earlier today, you will remember that one of the aims with a speculative letter is to ensure your details go into the right file. If your email isn't printed off then this of course won't happen. So the next time an interesting vacancy comes up your cover letter and CV won't be where you want them to be.

> ## Warning!
>
> Be aware that with emails busy people are very selective about what they print off. Whereas a reply to a job advertisement (one where you've been asked to submit the application by email) will be printed off, the same can't be said for a speculative enquiry. There is also the danger of your carefully crafted email being treated as spam, i.e. being deleted without being read, or, worse still, the file attachment with your CV not being opened because of concerns about unleashing viruses into the business's IT systems. We know of some organizations where emails with attachments from unknown people are filtered out automatically.

Don't expect a reply

One of the difficulties about sending off speculative job applications is that often you hear nothing back – not even an acknowledgement.

Whether employers should reply to everyone who sends in an unsolicited letter and CV is a matter of opinion. Some do, some don't, and this is a fact you are going to have to learn to live with. The biggest difficulty, of course, is not knowing whether your enquiry has been favourably received or not, whether it has been filed away in the right file or whether it has been fed into the shredding machine. In short, you get no feedback and this is the issue we will be dealing with next.

What is success?

With jobs which have been advertised, success can be judged by how many times you get on the interview list. However, with speculative job applications, measuring success isn't quite so easy. If your application has landed on the right desk at the right time and been favourably received, then you will probably find out by getting a phone call. If, on the other hand, you hear nothing then it could mean:

- **either** your application has been favourably received but the employer has no vacancies
- **or** your application has not been favourably received and it has gone somewhere it will never see the light of day again.

Focus on what's important

When evaluating the success of unsolicited cover letters, don't base your judgements on how many polite letters of acknowledgement you receive. Focus instead on what really matters, which is:

- connecting with opportunities which haven't yet surfaced on the job market
- making sure unadvertised opportunities never surface because you got in first.

Example of a cover letter for attacking the invisible market

Sharon Smart is in a sales job with a firm of distributors which services builders' merchants, DIY chains and garden centres. Sharon has seen her promotion prospects taken away by the appointment of a Sales Manager from outside the business. Being ambitious, she decides to see what the competition has to offer.

Sharon Smart
9 Quayside House
Nowhereville
WWxx xxx
Tel: xxxx xxxxxx
Mobile: xxxxx xxxxxx
email – sharonsmart@xxx.com

29 March 2013

CONFIDENTIAL

Jill Cleverly
Head of Sales
ABC Limited
Greenfield Industrial Estate
Greatly on Spree
GSXX XXX

Dear Jill Cleverly

Sales Management Opportunities

I am currently employed by Allproducts Distribution Services and I am writing to see if you have any openings in sales management for an ambitious twenty-nine-year-old graduate with five years' experience in the industry. My main reasons for feeling I am ready for a management position are:

- I spent three and a half years working a territory before being promoted into a key accounts role (the job I do now).
- The business I currently bring in accounts for approximately 30% of Allproducts' UK turnover.

- I am currently studying part-time for an MBA – a course I am on track to complete in six months' time.

A copy of my CV is attached.

I am available for interview at any time. My contractual period of notice is one month. My salary is £xxxxx per annum.

Yours sincerely

Sharon Smart

Attached: CV

Key points to pick out from Sharon Smart's cover letter are:

- It looks professional.
- It is well written.
- It makes a good first impression.
- It is a quick and easy read.
- Sharon has written by name to the person responsible for hiring staff in sales.
- The mention of Allproducts' name in the first line of the letter will quickly grab attention.
- She has made her ambitions clear. No one reading her letter will misunderstand why she is writing.
- She has also flagged up her salary benchmark – again, to prevent any misunderstandings.
- She has engaged ABC Limited with what will interest them most: her knowledge of the industry and the key role she plays in generating sales for her employer.
- She has not fogged the message in the letter with any irrelevant information.
- Mentioning the MBA is another way of flagging up her ambitions. No one would read into her application that she is just looking for another sales job like the one she's got.

Conclusion

Today we have seen that designing a cover letter to attack the invisible market is a very different task from designing one to apply for a job you've seen advertised. With the latter the stimulus comes from the employer whereas with the former the stimulus comes from you. This is why it is important you make it clear to employers why you are writing to them.

Speculative cover letters can sometimes seem like a lot of effort for little return but what needs to be remembered is that if you do connect with an opportunity:

- there's a good chance it hasn't been advertised
- you may have got in before the competition arrives.

Focussing on the second of these two bullet points, the issue of what makes you different from other applicants doesn't arise in these situations but the challenge you do face is finding out enough about the employers to know what will interest them. Where the recipient of your letter isn't in the same line of business you may have to work a little harder to find the common threads that will draw you together.

Fact-check (answers at the back)

1. What is the invisible job market?
   a) Another name for the old boy network ❑
   b) Jobs which aren't advertised ❑
   c) Jobs on the black economy ❑
   d) Jobs on short-term contracts ❑

2. What is the biggest plus point with jobs you source on the invisible market?
   a) They're better paid ❑
   b) You don't have to submit a full CV ❑
   c) You can pick and choose when you go for an interview ❑
   d) Less or no competition ❑

3. Why is it important to find out more about employers before you write to them?
   a) You'll learn more about what they will find interesting ❑
   b) You can find out which ones reply and which ones don't ❑
   c) You can find out who pays the best salaries ❑
   d) To avoid time-wasters ❑

4. With speculative cover letters whom is it best to write to?
   a) The Chief Executive ❑
   b) The Human Resources Manager ❑
   c) The person responsible for hiring people like you ❑
   d) The company, i.e. not a named individual ❑

5. With speculative cover letters, why is it important to be explicit about the kind of opportunities you are seeking?
   a) It makes a good impression ❑
   b) It makes you sound focussed and ambitious ❑
   c) It makes you sound assertive ❑
   d) Employers won't know otherwise and misunderstandings might creep in ❑

6. What's the point of writing 'confidential' on the envelope containing your cover letter and CV?
   a) To stop nosey people reading it ❑
   b) To make it sound important ❑
   c) It's a way of making sure it's opened by the right person ❑
   d) It creates a good first impression ❑

7. Why is it best to put a speculative cover letter in the post rather than sending it by email?
   a) It might be treated as spam ❑
   b) It creates a better impression ❑
   c) It might not be printed off ❑
   d) You're more likely to get a reply to a letter ❑

8. Why is it best to send out speculative cover letters in small batches?
a) It's easier ☐
b) It avoids you being asked to attend too many interviews at the same time ☐
c) It is less stressful ☐
d) You won't make as many spelling mistakes ☐

9. What is it best to do when you don't get a reply to a speculative cover letter?
a) Complain ☐
b) Ring up and find out why ☐
c) Post your opinion of the employer's bad manners on a social networking site ☐
d) Nothing ☐

10. What's the aim of sending out speculative cover letters?
a) Sourcing jobs which haven't been advertised ☐
b) Sourcing jobs which have been advertised but which are still vacant ☐
c) Encouraging employers to find a slot for you ☐
d) All three of the above ☐

FRIDAY

Cover letters for consultants

One way of attacking the invisible market is to get someone else to do it for you.

Today we will be looking at the task a cover letter has to perform when its purpose is to get you on the books of an employment agency. We will start by giving you an insight into how recruitment businesses work and what drives the people who work in them. We will see how pressure to get sales is a significant motivator and how, to get results, you need to harness this driving force.

A lot of what we will be doing today will be about making sure recruitment consultants understand you and how the responsibility of making this happen falls on you. A cover letter has an important part to play not only in making your ambitions clear but also in getting your relationship with a recruitment consultant off to a good start. If you tell them in clear unambiguous language what you want them to do for you then it stands a reasonable chance they will come up with the goods. If you don't then all kinds of misunderstandings can creep in, meaning your time on the agency's books will probably have nothing to show for it.

How consultants operate

One hard fact about agencies is they vary enormously in terms of both:

- their size
- their competence and professionalism.

Size isn't everything

Just because an agency is one of the well-known names doesn't necessarily mean it will be any good when it comes to finding you the job of your dreams. Small agencies, where often you find the consultant you're dealing with is one of the principals in the business, can and do perform very effectively.

No placement no fee

Agencies make their money out of successful placements. They place someone in a job and, when they do, they charge the employer a fee. How much do agencies charge employers? Fee structures vary but usually an employer would be looking at paying somewhere between 15 and 25 per cent of annual

starting salary. Sometimes, depending on the seniority of the position, agencies' fees can be much higher. Conversely agencies who do a lot of business with a given employer often apply discounts. Some part of the fee is usually reimbursable if for any reason the employer and the person who has been placed part company in the first few weeks.

What drives consultants?

With the fortunes of agencies tied entirely to how many candidates they are successful in placing, it is perhaps not surprising to find that recruitment consultants are usually incentivized by having a large part of their salary paid in commission. Equally, perhaps it is not surprising to find that this arrangement brings out the best and the worst in people. On the one hand it is good to see consultants focussed on using their skills to get people like you the jobs they want. On the other it can and does lead to consultants putting sales in front of everything and, it has to be said, in front of what could be your best interests. In practical terms it means:

- Candidates who are seen as easy to place get the most attention.
- Candidates who aren't get put to one side.
- In the enthusiasm to chalk up sales, the finer points in candidates' instructions sometimes get overlooked.

To illustrate what we mean by the last of these bullet points let's hear what Eric has to say about his experience of dealing with an agency.

Eric

I am an electrical engineer with a lot of hands-on experience of maintaining high-speed PLC-controlled machinery of the kind found in the food-processing and packaging industry. I have reached the point in my career where I am looking to move into a more technical role – for example in research and development. With this in mind I registered with a firm of recruitment consultants who, according to what they say about themselves on their website, specialize in technical appointments. Imagine, therefore, my disappointment when they started ringing me up every few days with jobs in maintenance which had just come onto their books. Every time I spoke to a different person. Every time I had to tell them I didn't want a job in maintenance. Every time they apologized and said they understood but the calls kept coming till in the end I got fed up and told them not to ring me any more.

Understanding consultants

So what are we looking at here? Incompetence? Laziness? People who don't listen? People who style themselves as experts but who don't have a clue? Or was Eric to blame in any way?

Recruitment consultants come in all shapes and sizes. Some are good, some are not so good, and you need to take these variations into account when you sit down to the job of designing a cover letter to send to the ones you have chosen. Most importantly, with recruitment consultants you need to understand:

● who they are
● where they're coming from
● what they do.

Given this understanding, you stand a good chance of getting on with them. Without it you could end up like Eric.

Where agencies fit into the job market

Let's look next at where agencies fit into the job market. Apart from supplying temps (which most of them do), what function do they perform and why do employers use them? Here are three examples of employers who have decided to use recruitment consultants, in each case for different reasons.

Employer A

'In the build up to the half year accounts, our Head of Finance suddenly decided she was going to leave. Faced with the need to get someone on board quickly, we rang up three firms of recruitment consultants who specialize in financial appointments to see if they had anyone on their books who might fit the bill.'

Employer B

'Our experience with advertising for staff has been poor. We find we spend a lot of money on advertisements, then in most cases the people who apply are totally unsuitable. What we have done recently is run our vacancies through a few firms of recruitment consultants to see who is on their files. OK, it's an expensive way to hire staff but at least we don't have to pay until we've taken someone on.'

Employer C

'We don't have the time or resources to sift through hundreds of job applications. We prefer to hand over our vacancies to firms of recruitment consultants and let them come up with a short list for us. It costs but in our view it's worth it.'

Points to pick out from these three examples are:

- How employers in a hurry are attracted to using consultants. A file search can usually be carried out within hours of a request being made. This contrasts favourably with advertising, with which it can take weeks to arrive at a short list.
- How 'no placement no fee' enables employers to see who is available on the market without it costing them anything.
- How consultants offer a solution to overstretched, lean-look organizations, which are typical of today.

> ## Key point
>
> Dealing with consultants can be painful but, as the three examples demonstrate, they can provide an important means of access to an area of the job market which would otherwise be closed to you. The challenge with consultants is in getting them to perform for you, and we will be seeing shortly how the design of your cover letter has an important part to play in addressing this challenge.

Consultants' files

The more candidates consultants have on file the better their chances are of:

- finding suitable people to match their clients' needs
- offering their clients a choice
- making money for themselves.

The need to get as many candidates on file as they can explains the lengths consultants go to get people to register with them.

The sheer volume of people on file, particularly with the larger agencies, presents the first challenge to you. When the right job comes along, what can you do to make sure it's your name that comes out in the file search?

A further factor to bear in mind here is that file search in a lot of consultancies is done by computer. A possible explanation for Eric's bad experience is that a file search carried out by computer was matching him up with jobs which didn't interest him – a problem we will be returning to later.

What you want your cover letter to do for you

So, to summarize, when you sign on with a firm of recruitment consultants, the task you want your cover letter to perform is to ensure:

- your name comes out in the file searches
- you connect with the right opportunities.

Your CV has the same task to perform too but remember:

- It's your cover letter that's read first.
- What's read first makes the biggest and most lasting impression.

Three assumptions

When you sit down to the job of designing a cover letter to send to a firm of recruitment consultants it is useful to start by making three fairly safe assumptions:

1 The point we have touched on already. Any agency you make contact with will be heavily results orientated. Your value in their eyes will be governed by one fact alone: whether they can place you in a job or not.

2 An agency is a busy place where new candidates are registering all the time. What this means is that your cover letter and CV will be subject to bulk processing, whereby once again the messages in them will need to satisfy the 'one quick read' test. They must be capable of being understood instantly because, if they're not, they could end up in the wrong part of the databank (another possible explanation for what happened to Eric).

3 Some of the tasks in an agency will be performed by people who have little or no understanding of what you do or the terminology you use.

Pick out your marketable talents

Focussing on what makes you attractive to recruitment consultants (what gets their blood racing), you need to use your cover letter to highlight anything in your qualifications, skills and experience which will make you marketable to their clients. Since you don't know their clients, this takes you back to fishing in the dark. The only clue you have is by looking again at why employers use recruitment consultants and going back to the three examples we used earlier.

- **Scarce skills and unusual experience.** Identify any scarce skills you may have or unusual areas of experience. Employers often go to recruitment consultants because they feel that (a) they're looking for someone special and (b) other methods of recruitment won't work for them. Is there anything in your portfolio which marks you out as different from most people in your profession? If there is, then make sure it is highlighted in your cover letter. For example, Shah is a management accountant but, because of his company's corporate development strategies, he has had more involvement with mergers and acquisitions than most people with his background.
- **Competence in core areas.** Employers who go to recruitment consultants are often looking for a safe pair of hands – for example, someone to steady the ship after a turbulent period or, as in the case of Employer A, someone stable and reliable to take over from a key member of staff who has departed unexpectedly and at a critical time. Such employers will be briefing consultants to come up with the names of candidates who are competent in the core areas of their job by virtue of their experience.

> ## Key point
> These marketable talents are the ones you need to bring into prominence when you design a cover letter for consultants.

Make sure consultants understand you

It is important consultants understand you because, as we saw in the case of Eric, they have a tendency to lock onto any talents they see as marketable and then, unless directed otherwise, pepper candidates with everything that comes onto the books which loosely seems to match those talents. Why is this a problem?

- Candidates' instructions can get ignored and in this way they gain no benefit from registering with the consultant. In Eric's case all he heard about was jobs in maintenance – jobs which didn't interest him.

- Sooner or later consultants get fed up with candidates who keep saying 'no'. They detach their effort. The calls stop.

How to get the message across

Your cover letter is the ideal place for you to tell consultants what you want them to do for you. How to do this?

- Don't use jargon because, unless the agency is specialized, the people who read your cover letter may not understand you.
- Keep the messages as plain, short and simple as you can. Reduce the possibility of misunderstandings.
- Be precise. Say exactly what you want and don't leave anything to the imagination.

Remember what you are trying to achieve here. If a job comes into the consultant's office which is right up your street, you want to be sure you trigger the retrieval systems. The file search has got to throw out your name.

Tip: key words
If you have ever had any input into the design of a website you will know the importance of key words – words which search engines hook onto and bring visitors to your site. See your cover letters to consultants as a bit like selecting key words with the consultants in the place of search engines. For example, in Shah's case, 'mergers and acquisitions' are key words which he could even highlight in bold so no one misses them. Note: don't overdo the highlighting in bold or it defeats the object.

Don't register with too many agencies

Registering with too many agencies can give you two problems:

- being asked to attend too many interviews at the same time, leaving you with the problem of getting time off work
- two or more agencies putting you forward for the same job.

One size does fit all

Contrary to everything we've said so far this week, the task of designing a cover letter for one agency is no different from designing a cover letter for another. Here is where you can use a standard model; in other words, there is no need to customize each letter.

Example of a cover letter for consultants

Robin Wrightly is a human resources manager in a business which is due to close in six months' time. Robin is emailing his CV to a consultant with one of the leading names in executive recruitment in the area where he lives.

To: Tim Fotheringay
From: Robin Wrightly
Subject: CV
Date: 29 March 2013

Dear Tim Fotheringay

I am seeking a position in human resources management paying £xx,xxx per annum plus and would like to be considered for any suitable opportunities.

From my CV (attached) you will see I have worked in all areas of HR including:

- pay negotiations with six unions representing staff and manual grades
- a 90% success rate in defending employment tribunal cases
- managing a programme of change which included new shift patterns and payment systems affecting over 200 employees.

I am available to attend interviews at any time. The unit where I am based is scheduled for closure in six months' time, which means all employees on site including myself are at risk of redundancy. Early release would be available to me if I was

---

successful in finding alternative employment. If you require any other information at this stage please do not hesitate to ask.

Yours sincerely

Robin Wrightly
Attached: CV

Key points to pick out from Robin's email are as follows:

- It is concise and to the point. No space is wasted on information which isn't relevant.
- In his first paragraph Robin makes it clear exactly what kind of position he is seeking and where his salary expectations lie.
- From his experience he has picked out three areas which he thinks will make him more marketable.
- He has recognized that not being able to start a job for six months might detract from his marketability. He has therefore included the few words about the availability of early release.

Conclusion

Today we have been looking at designing a cover letter to use when registering with an agency. Here the challenge you face is engaging with the forces which drive recruitment consultants, namely:

- success in terms of placements
- the financial rewards that go with it.

Today we have asked you to focus on your marketable talents because these offer the key as far as consultants are concerned. They will see you as someone they can sell to their clients and make money out of, this will fire their efforts to give their best for you.

Also today we have stressed the need to send consultants off on the track you want them to follow and not one dictated by their ambition to chalk up more sales. Making it clear to consultants at the outset what you want them to do for you is an important element of getting off on the right foot with them and you can do this in your cover letter.

Finally, when you're dealing with consultants, expect to have to remind them about your aims from time to time because, they are apt to forget.

SUNDAY MONDAY TUESDAY WEDNESDAY THURSDAY FRIDAY SATURDAY

Fact-check (answers at the back)

1. What is 'no placement no fee'?
   a) An arrangement whereby you don't have to pay the agency any money if they don't find a job for you ❏
   b) An arrangement whereby the employer doesn't have to pay the agency any money until someone starts in a job ❏
   c) An arrangement whereby the agency agrees to work for free ❏
   d) An arrangement whereby the agency is paid up front ❏

2. How do agencies make money?
   a) They are subsidized by the government ❏
   b) They charge fees to people who register with them ❏
   c) Employers pay them retainers ❏
   d) They charge fees to employers when they place people with them ❏

3. From a job hunter's perspective, where do agencies score?
   a) They access areas of the job market which would otherwise be closed to you ❏
   b) They write cover letters and CVs for you ❏
   c) They don't score. They're a waste of space ❏
   d) They have access to better-paid jobs ❏

4. What is the danger if you fail to give agencies a specification to work to?
   a) They won't ring you ❏
   b) They'll come up with the wrong jobs ❏
   c) They'll refer you to a careers counsellor ❏
   d) They'll put your CV in the shredding machine ❏

5. What will impress agencies most?
   a) Outstanding academic achievements ❏
   b) Your IT skills ❏
   c) Talents that they can market to their clients ❏
   d) Your references ❏

6. Why do agencies want people to register with them?
   a) To attract government grants ❏
   b) To keep them busy ❏
   c) To draw visitors onto their websites ❏
   d) So they will have more people on their files ❏

7. When can you use the same cover letter more than once?
   a) When you're in a hurry ❏
   b) When you're registering with agencies ❏
   c) When you're writing off for places on graduate intakes ❏
   d) When the job is with an employer you've written to before ❏

8. What is the danger if you keep saying you're not interested in the jobs agencies find for you?
a) They might charge you for wasting their time ❏
b) They might put you on a black list ❏
c) There is no danger (you're entitled to say you're not interested) ❏
d) They lose interest in you ❏

9. When dealing with agencies, what is one of the drawbacks with saying you're looking for an exceptionally high salary?
a) They may see you as someone who is going to be difficult to place ❏
b) You might look greedy ❏
c) No one will take you seriously ❏
d) You might look like someone who's just shopping round to see what's out there ❏

10. How do you judge the effectiveness of an agency?
a) By the number of times they phone you ❏
b) By the enthusiasm of their consultants ❏
c) By what they have to say about themselves on their websites ❏
d) By the number of interesting job opportunities they come up with ❏

SATURDAY

Moving into the future

On Monday we looked at how cover letters:

- are not just there to get you interviews
- go on working for you as the selection process moves forward.

Today we will take a closer look at how cover letters can influence:

- the directions interviews go in
- final selection decisions.

Also today we will look at how you can learn from your job applications and get better at writing cover letters. Yes, practice does make perfect, but the confidence and style with which you write can play an important part in your life, which goes a long way beyond how good you are at turning out cover letters. We will look at what you can take forward from the experience of writing a cover letter. We will therefore see how you can apply what you have learned to writing the other letters you will need to, as the selection process advances. At the same time we will see how judgments of people are formed based on their ability to express themselves clearly and how, in an age when so much communication is done online, the need to write well is arguably more important than it has ever been.

Interviews

Imagine the scene. You have been asked to attend an interview, so along you go not exactly sure what to expect. The interviewer is usually sitting behind a desk and, in most cases, it will be someone you've never met before. Indeed, up to this point the interviewer's knowledge of you will be based almost entirely on what you've said about yourself in:

- your cover letter
- your CV
- your application form (if you've been asked to fill one in).

Interestingly, these documents will probably be sitting on the desk in front of the interviewer with your cover letter uppermost because, if you've been following the advice so far, you will have designed your cover letter so it is effectively the first page of your CV.

Interview questions

What candidates sometimes forget is that they may have more experience of interviews than the person who is interviewing them. And, when all is said and done, interviewing a complete stranger for a job can be a daunting task, especially to someone who isn't used to it. Many line managers have had no formal training in interviewing beyond perhaps going on the odd short course. What's more, they only occasionally get the chance to practice their interviewing skills (when there is a vacancy for staff in the area of the business they control). The result in many cases is an interviewer who is not too sure about what line of questioning to follow and so the natural inclination is to be led by what's in front of them – namely your cover letter.

Dictate the agenda

The information in your cover letter backed up by the more detailed information in your CV can determine to a large extent:

- the direction interviews take
- the topics that come up for discussion
- the questions that are asked.

So what we are seeing here is how a carefully crafted cover letter can have the power to dictate the agenda for an interview and, more to the point perhaps, an agenda which will be favourable to you, the applicant. Everything in your cover letter will be:

- relevant to the job for which you are being interviewed
- one of your strong points.

Straightaway the interview gets off to a good start, and the more time spent on talking about what makes you a great candidate for the job, clearly the better it is going to be for you.

The halo effect again

We looked at the halo effect on Sunday. Just to remind you, the halo effect is where:

● a candidate makes a good first impression
● any flaws which emerge later are ignored

Interviewers – particularly inexperienced ones – are very susceptible to halo effects. They make their minds up about candidates in the first few minutes and anything later on in the interview which doesn't fit in with the already formed favourable opinion will be either overlooked or relegated in importance.

Keeping copies of your cover letters

Some candidates put a lot of time and effort into rehearsing answers to tough interview questions which they think they are going to be asked. Where proportionately less time and effort is spent is on the job of revisiting the cover letter, CV and application form which they sent in. A pity? Yes it is, because, following on from the last point, by looking at what they said about themselves they might learn a lot more about the line of questioning they are going to face.

An even bigger pity would be if for any reason they hadn't kept copies of these documents because:

- they didn't save them
- they overwrote them
- they didn't run off hard copies.

> ## Key point
>
> Always run off a hard copy of anything you send to an employer, including your cover letter. Keep the hard copy with everything else to do with your application, in a separate folder for each job

Consistency and credibility

You will remember that on Monday we warned you about the importance of consistency between any information you put in a cover letter and any information you put in a CV. The point applies equally to interviews. Anything you say at an interview (for example, in response to a question you are asked) needs to be consistent with what you have said in your cover letter, in your CV and on any application forms you have been asked to fill in. This emphasizes again the importance of revisiting these documents before you go to your interviews and reminding yourself exactly what you did say. Remember: your credibility is at stake here and, once you lose it, it won't be easy to get back.

What went wrong?

Candidates go for interviews, psych themselves up before they go and feel at the end of it they've put in a good performance. Then they get a letter or an email telling them they haven't been shortlisted. 'What went wrong?' they ask themselves.

'Did I put my foot in it and, if so, where?' Here the answer could lie in something they said at the interview which:

- was at odds with information they had given elsewhere
- caused the interviewer to think twice.

Learn from the experience

Applying for a job – irrespective of whether your application is successful or not – is an experience from which you can learn valuable lessons.

In the case of cover letters, some people will have little difficulty in applying what they have learned this week, whereas others may struggle. Expressing yourself concisely doesn't come easily to everyone because, when you're talking about a subject which is familiar to you (such as your work), it is a great temptation to stray off the point and go into detail. This is fine where the detail is relevant – for example, in a competitive job situation, where it highlights something about you which makes you stand out from other applicants. However, if this isn't the case then your long rambling explanations will only serve to lose the reader's interest.

The art of précis

A précis is a short summary of a piece of writing. It gives the bare bones and nothing more. Someone reading a précis will see at a glance what the piece is about and, if it looks interesting, they will read it in full.

See a cover letter as an exercise in précis, in this case a précis of the **relevant** information in your CV. Pick out the main points, put to one side anything which isn't relevant and then say what you want to say in the smallest number of words possible.

Perfect the art of précis

It is easy to perfect précis. Take an article in a magazine or newspaper and sum up what it's about in three or four short sentences.

Writing a précis is an excellent exercise for:

- increasing your vocabulary
- improving your grammar and spelling
- expressing yourself clearly and concisely
- making you think.

Take the lessons forward

What can you take forward from the experience of writing a cover letter? How else can you apply what you have learned?

A cover letter isn't, of course, going to be the only letter you will need as the selection process advances. All being well, you will be invited to attend an interview and, if the interview goes to plan, you will be asked to go back for another one and/or at some point offered the job.

At each of these stages you may be called on to write a letter either to confirm you will be attending the interview or to say you will be accepting the job. All the etiquette you learned about on Tuesday will come into play again. However, do please note the following:

- If you're invited to an interview or offered a job, always remember to say thank you.
- Always reply to letters/emails using the same terms of address as the writer's. For example, if they address you as 'Dear Mr/Mrs/Ms', do likewise when you reply to them. If on the other hand they're less formal (e.g. in an email, 'Hi' followed by your first name) then it's acceptable to write back in the same style.

Does it matter?

We pose this question because there are a lot of people out there who take the view that it doesn't matter if letters and emails are poorly written and/or full of bad grammar and spelling mistakes. So long as the people they've written to understand them, why get hung up about the odd bad construction or apostrophe in the wrong place?

Putting to one side the fact that badly written letters often don't make sense to the people who have to read them, the bigger point here is that the way you express yourself in written form is an extension of who you are. If your letters are ill constructed and messy, that's the image of you they project. If – as we mentioned earlier in the book – they're littered with silly mistakes then the image of you that comes across is that of someone who's slipshod and careless.

Using your writing style to project the right image

We are, as we know, living in an increasingly image-conscious world, but what you also need to remember here is that:

● More and more business is conducted in written form thanks to email and other online forms of communication.
● Less and less revolves around the use of the spoken word, either face-to-face or over the phone.

A large part of the image we project today is, therefore, determined by what we put into writing and how we say it. Writing which is snappy and straight to the point comes across as an outward manifestation of an organized and tidy mind, whereas writing which is messy and all over the place comes across as the exact opposite.

Warning!

Don't fall into the trap of thinking 'anything goes' just because you're saying it in an email. The standards of good business letter writing go right across the board. Bear in mind, too, that to be good and well-written doesn't mean it has to be stiff and formal. At the same time, don't lapse into the kind of conversational style which may be acceptable in emails to your friends and family. Equally, don't give business emails the same treatment as posting messages on social networking sites (another common fault). Remember, it's your image we're talking about here and you're the one who's responsible for it.

Build your self-confidence

So far this week we have portrayed people who can't put together a decent cover letter as people who either can't be bothered to go to the trouble or people who are careless and don't check their work. There is, however, another group of people who find having to put anything into writing daunting and something which they would prefer to avoid if at all possible. The problem in many of these cases is not bad teaching in the schools they attended but lack of self-confidence.

Designing a cover letter may be a small step to take but when your self-confidence is low:

- It is a step.
- It is one going in the right direction.

Earlier this week we drew your attention to the link between a well-written letter and confidence in what the writer is saying. Someone who can express themselves clearly and in a well-thought-out manner is someone who has something important to say. Readers sit up and take notice, and being taken seriously in this way is a great boost to self-confidence.

Note

Even where self-confidence isn't a problem, the ability to communicate effectively in writing is a mark of quality which your bosses and colleagues will be quick to notice. In terms of your career prospects it will do you nothing but good.

Give the job the respect it deserves

Writing a good cover letter, picking out from your skills, experience and qualifications what's relevant to each job application you make and then linking these points together in a clear and concise fashion is something you can get better at. Partly this is a case of practice makes perfect, but that is not the whole story. What is equally and possibly more important is treating the job of writing a good cover letter with the respect it deserves. Even today, when most job seekers are clued up about what to do and have a lot of expert advice available to them, the cover letter is still the poor relation when it comes to presenting an employer with a set of credentials which will impress them. Still we find cover letters coming in which look as if they have been dashed off in ten minutes (or less) and – the point we made at the start of the week – show little evidence of having the same care and attention lavished on them as the CVs which accompany them. All of which brings us back to the point about the important part cover letters have to play in:

● getting CVs read
● moving job applications forward in the right direction.

The message? Attach proper importance to the job of writing a cover letter. Give it your best shot and not some half-hearted effort which will inspire no one to take an interest in you.

Conclusion

Today we have discovered how a good cover letter isn't just one which gets you interviews. Far from it: as you move into the future it goes on working for you in ways which may surprise you:

- It can dictate what happens at an interview and lay down an agenda which will be favourable to you.
- It can prepare you for other letters you may have to write as the selection process moves forward.
- It can teach you how to express yourself clearly and concisely in writing.
- It can help you project an image which is consistent with someone who is organized and businesslike.
- It can help you to build your self-confidence.

The final message today was to attach importance to the job of composing a cover letter. Put time and effort into it and take pride in it when you get it right. If you do, it will pay you back with interest and all the time and effort will then be worth it.

SUNDAY MONDAY TUESDAY WEDNESDAY THURSDAY FRIDAY SATURDAY

Fact-check (answers at the back)

1. Why do some interviewers find interviews daunting?
   a) Because they don't know how to handle applicants ❑
   b) Because they're not used to doing them ❑
   c) Because they're useless ❑
   d) Because they've had no training ❑

2. Why is it important to keep copies of your cover letters?
   a) So you can use them again next time you apply for a job ❑
   b) So you have proof you wrote one ❑
   c) As a memento of all the effort you put into writing them ❑
   d) So you can remind yourself what you said before you go for an interview ❑

3. What is a précis?
   a) A short summary of a piece of writing ❑
   b) Another name for a CV ❑
   c) A French word for an interview ❑
   d) Where there is a match between the requirements of the job and what you have to offer ❑

4. When does conforming to good business letter-writing standards not matter?
   a) In emails ❑
   b) On Fridays ❑
   c) When you're not on business ❑
   d) When you're in a hurry ❑

5. Why is it important to aspire to a good standard of business letter writing?
   a) It isn't important any more (it went out with the Ark) ❑
   b) It projects a good image ❑
   c) It shows you've been to university ❑
   d) It keeps you out of trouble with your bosses ❑

6. How can you get better at writing cover letters?
   a) By applying for more jobs ❑
   b) By getting someone else to write them for you ❑
   c) By using specimens downloaded off the Internet ❑
   d) By attaching greater importance to them ❑

7. Apart from confirming you will be attending, what is it important to say when you reply to an invitation to an interview?
   a) To allow you five minutes in case you arrive late ❑
   b) Get out the red carpet ❑
   c) Thank you ❑
   d) That you will want to be reimbursed for your travelling expenses ❑

8. Why is good business letter writing becoming more important?
   a) The litigation culture and the need to put everything into writing so you can prove what you said in court ❏
   b) Because of the increasing use of online communication ❏
   c) It's cheaper to write than it is to make a phone call ❏
   d) People don't do anything unless you put it into writing ❏

9. What can you learn from writing a good cover letter?
   a) How to express yourself clearly and concisely ❏
   b) How to write a CV ❏
   c) How to make friends with people who don't know you ❏
   d) How to be brilliant at everything ❏

10. What makes writing a good cover letter difficult?
    a) Not having sufficient confidence in yourself ❏
    b) Not having a good education ❏
    c) Not applying for jobs very often ❏
    d) Nothing does. It isn't difficult ❏

7 × 7

1 Seven good habits

- Proofread everything carefully.
- Use a dictionary. Don't rely on spell checkers.
- Pay attention to detail.
- Make the effort when it comes to matching your skills, experience and qualifications to the requirements of a job.
- Remember to sign any cover letters you put in the post.
- Never undersell yourself. See where you have something special to offer and make sure everybody knows about it.
- Learn from experience.

2 Seven key messages

- Cover letters are what employers read first. The impression they make is one that lasts.
- Design a new cover letter every time you apply for a job. Make sure everything you put in it is relevant.
- Cover letters designed to attack the visible job market need to address the issue of engaging and overcoming competition.
- A good cover letter carries on working for you right the way through to the final stages of selection.
- Have something positive to say to employers about why you want to work for them.
- With speculative cover letters it's you not the employer who designs the job specification; it's you who has to tell the employer what you're looking for.
- Treat the job of writing a cover letter with the respect it deserves.

3 Seven surprising facts

- The number of cover letters riddled with mistakes that are written by well qualified professionals.
- How many CVs are binned before they're read because the cover letters that come with them contained nothing relevant or interesting.
- How often a CV which has had a lot of thought put into its preparation is accompanied by a cover letter which has the appearance of being dashed off in five minutes.
- Cover letters aren't always read from start to finish.
- How many cover letters arrive with the names of people they're addressed to spelled incorrectly.
- How many well-qualified candidates fall by the wayside because they fail to pay sufficient attention to their cover letters.
- How many candidates send in CVs without a cover letter. How they miss a great opportunity.

4 Seven things to avoid

- Inconsistencies in the information you give to employers of the sort that will serve to undermine your credibility.
- Cluttering your cover letters with information that isn't relevant.
- Making your cover letter uninviting to read by trying to cram too much information on the page.
- Sending a cover letter without a date on it.
- Using capital (upper case) letters, underlining or picking out key words in red.
- Forgetting to sign cover letters you're putting in the post.
- Allowing the standards to lapse when you're submitting a cover letter by email.

5 Seven things to do today

- Ditch any standard templates you've been using.
- Read up on apostrophes. Make sure you know when and when not to use them.
- Write a short précis. Pick an article you have seen in a newspaper or on a website and summarize it in two or three paragraphs.
- Check your stock of A4 paper and envelopes. Make sure you've got a spare cartridge for your printer.
- Let someone who is qualified (e.g. a secretary) have a look at a sample of your typing. Satisfy yourself it comes up to acceptable business standards.
- Play a word game.
- Start taking a pride in anything you write.

6 Seven top tips

- See a good cover letter as the best way of creating a favourable first impression.
- Keep your cover letters concise. Achieve conciseness by making sure everything in them is relevant to the job for which you're applying.
- When submitting your CV in a file attachment to an email, include a copy of your cover letter in the same file.
- Keep your sentences short so the meaning of what you're saying is clear. Write the way you speak when you're designing a cover letter. Aim to be businesslike but, at the same time, engaging and friendly.
- With speculative cover letters, always send them to the person responsible for hiring people like you. Put them in an envelope marked 'confidential'.
- Always keep copies of cover letters you send to employers. Don't delete or write over them in case you're invited to an interview and you need to remind yourself what you said.
- See a good cover letter as what can make the difference when you're up against stiff competition.

7 Seven trends for tomorrow

- Employers and employers' organizations will continue to wage war on job applicants who can't spell. Expect more from prominent business leaders.
- A greater tendency for job applicants to use standard templates for cover letters thanks to the glut of material available on the Internet or from other sources; this gives an opportunity to people who can produce cover letters designed for purpose.
- In an online and image-conscious age the need to write well will command an ever-increasing level of importance.
- As the world of jobs becomes more competitive, a good cover letter could be what makes the difference.
- Greater focus on cover letters; more interest in what they say about the people who write them and their ability to communicate effectively and concisely.
- The trend of bringing cover letters and CVs together in one document is set to grow.
- Cover letters and CVs will increasingly be used by self-employed people as a way of selling their skills; a cover letter and a CV is a good way of advertising credentials to potential clients.

Answers

Sunday: 1c; 2c; 3c; 4b; 5d; 6a; 7d; 8b; 9b; 10c.

Monday: 1b; 2a; 3c; 4a; 5d; 6a; 7b; 8c; 9c; 10b.

Tuesday: 1d; 2b; 3a; 4d; 5c; 6b; 7c; 8c; 9a and c; 10b.

Wednesday: 1b; 2a; 3d; 4b; 5c; 6c; 7a; 8b; 9d; 10d.

Thursday: 1b; 2d; 3a; 4c; 5d; 6c; 7a and c; 8b; 9d; 10d.

Friday: 1b; 2d; 3a; 4b; 5c; 6d; 7b; 8d; 9a; 10d.

Saturday: 1b and d; 2d; 3a; 4c; 5b; 6d; 7c; 8b; 9a; 10d.

Notes

ALSO AVAILABLE IN THE 'IN A WEEK' SERIES

APPRAISALS • BRAND MANAGEMENT • BUSINESS PLANS • CONTENT MARKETING • COVER LETTERS • DIGITAL MARKETING • DIRECT MARKETING • EMOTIONAL INTELLIGENCE • FINDING & HIRING TALENT • JOB HUNTING • LEADING TEAMS • MARKET RESEARCH • MARKETING • MBA • MOBILE MARKETING • NETWORKING • OUTSTANDING CONFIDENCE • PEOPLE MANAGEMENT • PLANNING YOUR CAREER • PROJECT MANAGEMENT • SMALL BUSINESS MARKETING • STARTING A NEW JOB • TACKLING TOUGH INTERVIEW QUESTIONS • TIME MANAGEMENT

For information about other titles in the 'In A Week' series, please visit www.teachyourself.co.uk

MORE TITLES AVAILABLE IN THE 'IN A WEEK' SERIES

ADVANCED NEGOTIATION SKILLS • ASSERTIVENESS • BUSINESS ECONOMICS • COACHING • COPYWRITING • DECISION MAKING • DIFFICULT CONVERSATIONS • ECOMMERCE • FINANCE FOR NON-FINANCIAL MANAGERS • JOB INTERVIEWS • MANAGING STRESS AT WORK • MANAGING YOUR BOSS • MANAGING YOURSELF • MINDFULNESS AT WORK • NEGOTIATION SKILLS • NLP • PEOPLE SKILLS • PSYCHOMETRIC TESTING • SEO AND SEARCH MARKETING • SOCIAL MEDIA MARKETING • START YOUR OWN BUSINESS • STRATEGY • SUCCESSFUL SELLING • UNDERSTANDING AND INTERPRETING ACCOUNTS

For information about other titles in the 'In A Week' series, please visit www.teachyourself.co.uk

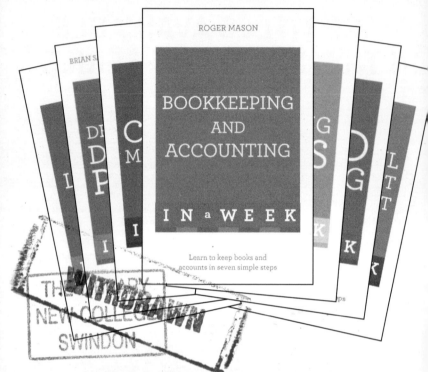

YOUR FASTEST ROUTE TO SUCCESS

LEARN IN A WEEK WHAT THE EXPERTS LEARN IN A LIFETIME

For information about other titles in the 'In A Week' series, please visit
www.teachyourself.co.uk